HOW TO DO PRACTICALLY ANYTHING
Trick, fool, bamboozle, confuse, confound, turn
the tables on, and generally freak out

TO PRACTICALLY ANYONE
Family, friends, teacher, bureaucrats, computer
nuts, and bosses, not to mention widows and
orphans

ON PRACTICALLY ANY OCCASION
Meals, parties, classtimes, office hours, weddings,
and (well, maybe not but why not) funerals

IN THE MOST PRACTICALLY PERFECT GUIDE
TO WINNING THE LAUGHTER GAME—

The Official Handbook
of Practical Jokes

D0047048

How to Construct Your Own Backyard Nuclear Reactor

Peter van der Linden

This unusual and pleasing book gives all the essential facts for the under-fives. It combines the experience of years with the enthusiasm of the man who put the "*boot*" in "*booty*." Read it now, and help the author **become fabulously rich.**

The Official Handbook of Practical Jokes

Peter van der Linden

A SIGNET BOOK

NEW AMERICAN LIBRARY

This book is intended for entertainment and humor purposes only. Neither the author nor the publisher can assume any responsibility for the use or misuse of any information contained within this book.

You are reading this book upside down.

Just kidding . . .

Acknowledgments

Most books start with a short, saccharine-sweet section where the author heaps praise and thanks on his colleagues, secretary, wife, mistress, parents, pets, and anyone who had a hand in the work. The author always ends by accepting sole responsibility for any remaining errors.

None of my relatives ever showed the least interest in the project. Since I don't have a wife or mistress, no thanks are due there either. My girlfriend was pretty unhelpful while I was trying to put these ideas together (pretty, but unhelpful). I personally carved the entire manuscript onto granite tablets. It was a tricky job cart, but at least the pages didn't get dog-eared. An additional benefit was that nobody ever used the manuscript to light a kitchen fire, although I did have to retrieve the chapter on college life from the southeast corner of a publisher's rock garden.

The fine products of the following companies helped to sustain author morale: the Myers Jamaican Rum Company, Baron Rothschild Vineyards, Jacques Hennesey Cognac Company, and the Miller Brewing Company (and what a hangover *that* was the next morning).

I haven't yet said anything about the people I asked to help me collect lists of practical jokes. If there are any remaining errors in the book, it is wholly the fault of these idle and slovenly people (and you know who you are).

Finally, I would like to humbly dedicate this book to the one person without whom it could never have been written: myself.

PvdL

Contents

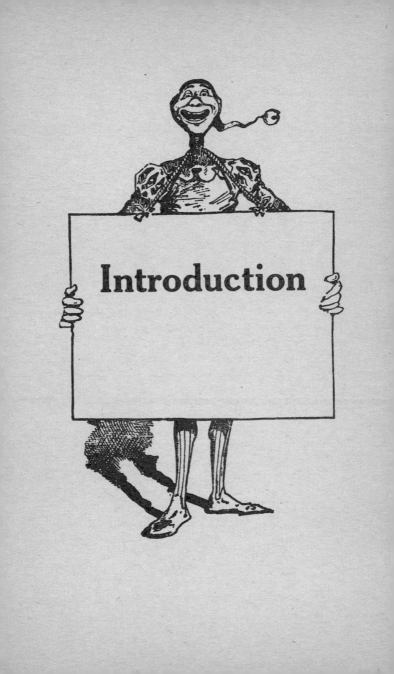

This wasn't the book I had in mind when I started. But I still remember the original concept as if I were working on it only last week. As a matter of fact, I *was* working on it only last week. This book is so fresh that if you hold a page up to your ear, you'll hear the ink drying. It all started like this. I was sitting in a grimy publisher's office (most publishers are grimy, due to their habit of holding books to their ears to check the freshness). I was describing my idea of a steamy exposé of the sordid life of a young, jet-setting single with more money than inhibitions.

Nothing was to be held back from the true story of my life. I began to outline the wild parties on board luxury yachts, the fast, sleek sports cars, and the even faster, sleeker, and sportier women. The beads of perspiration were running down the publisher's flushed face, forming a stalactite off his nose. You could see that he was very, very interested. "With latex and whipping cream, you say?" The publisher faltered and licked his lips. "When did all this debauchery take place?"

My reply was easy and to the point, but it appeared to kiss finis to the project. "As soon as you cough up the cash for the publication rights," I told him. I unexpectedly found myself being helped out of the office into the street by two large and kindly publisher's men. As I dusted off my jacket and picked myself up, the publisher poked his head out of the window several stories above. Returning my attaché case he followed it up with some piquant but well-meant advice to stick to things I knew about. I dodged the falling briefcase but followed the advice. So it was *sayonara* to the fast lane, but a hearty *bonjour* to practical jokers everywhere.

17

Everyone knows what a practical joke is, and most people enjoy a good one at somebody else's expense. A practical joke has two essential elements: a victim and an unexpected situation which confronts him to the amusement of everyone else.

Sex and Practical Jokes

Practical jokes are mostly played by men. It's not that women don't have a sense of humor, it's just that it's different than men's. Through the marvelous miracle of modern microsurgery, doctors have recently discovered the location of the sense of humor in the human body.

Previously thought to exist somewhere near the elbow or "funny bone," medical experts now state that the sense of humor is mostly located in the dong. Also, the humor gland which secretes dirty jokes is, in scientific terms, somewhere pretty darn near the family jewels.

This immediately explains why women often "don't get" jokes; possessing only a vestigial *schwanz*, the fairer sex has a correspondingly undeveloped sense of humor. Completely lacking *cojones*, most women find scatological humor totally incomprehensible.

Building on this amazing medical breakthrough, some researchers have proposed that the wanger is also the site of the sense of purpose, the sense of fair play, and the false sense of security.

But if the male alone is heir to these qualities, what might the female anatomy host? Preliminary investigation suggests a sense of frustration and the sixth sense. The sixth sense is that unerring power which enables a woman to detect instinctively the logic of an argument and thwart it by emotion. The sixth sense also acts as a homing device for locating shopping malls, garage sales, and especially for knowing when to buy more bathroom tissue. But it is totally dysfunctional as far as practical jokes are concerned.

Pay Attention to These Serious Warnings

Practical jokes must always be harmless and easily reversible, otherwise the prankster has strayed over the boundary into nuisance, which is not funny. Never do anything which is illegal or which might be dangerous. Never do anything which might injure or hurt someone.

The victim of a practical joke should be an extroverted person, capable of withstanding mild fun-poking. Generally the more self-assured the victim, the more hilarious it is to see him struggle with the outcome of some bizarre gag.

The element of surprise is important, together with an inclination to action rather than theory. My own preference is to not give away any hint that a prank is underway, until it has already climaxed. As well as heightening the dramatic tension, this also gives you the advantage of plausible deniability as used by governments throughout the free world. Practical jokes are therapeutic in that they cause amusement and help people to realize that life is more than an orderly progression of planned situations.

The humor comes from the victim's reaction to the off-beat circumstance in which he finds himself. Occasionally the humorous element arises because the victim does not even realize he is the object of a prank. When the light finally dawns, however, remember to reassure the victim that the surrounding group of snickering ninnies is "laughing *at* you, not *with* you."

Zingers and Boomerangs

There are two refinements to the basic practical joke: Zingers and Boomerangs. A Zinger is a follow-up to the basic prank, which yields exquisite extra satisfaction. For example, placing a fake stick-on water tap in an unlikely position (say the side of your television) is a simple basic prank. Adding a half-full glass of water beneath, so it looks like the tap is dripping, then sipping from the glass when someone comes into view, is a Zinger.

In contrast, a Boomerang is anything which makes a joke backfire and rebound on the player. For example, my friend Harris once secretly put a thin slice of carrot into a goldfish tank with the intention of later snatching it out and swallowing it, pretending it was a fish, to amaze the assembled company. Unfortunately, in the heat of the moment, Harris trawled the wrong object, and it's hard to say who was most amazed: Harris, the spectators, or the goldfish which he had scooped up. Try to avoid Boomerangs.

Designing Your Own Practical Jokes

Practical jokes are, above all else, practical. They are meant to be played and enjoyed. In this book I strike a balance between practical jokes which apply only to a unique situation, and practical jokes with a broad applicability which anyone can try for himself. The reader should be able to use about half of the jokes described here immediately and without any special adaption. The other pranks describe scenarios where the prankster took advantage of a specialized location, event, or circumstance.

People often ask where I get my ideas for practical jokes. Many practical jokes occur naturally; all the joker does is notice the basic situation and develop it slightly further than nature intended. For instance, if you have never seen popcorn being cooked, you would never imagine how it suddenly and violently erupts when it pops. Popcorn is not widely eaten outside the United States; and voilà, there you have the basics for a good trick to play on any European visits or visitors.

The facility comes with practice, and you eventually develop an eye for the off-beat situation, that unusual circumstance which forms the basis for a successful set-up. Do you have to be born a good creative practical joker, or is it something you can learn? Well, obviously it helps if you have designer genes, but even if you don't, there is hope for you. Experiment with the gimmick jokes first—revolving bow-ties, mustard jars with jumping snakes, pepper-flavored toffee, rubber pencils, fake insects, plastic barf, and so on. Even the Marquis de Sade (who was a renowned practical joker in his youth, before he fell in with the wrong crowd and got mixed up in local politics) had to start somewhere. A good place for a novice to start is with the chapter entitled "The Joy of Junk."

It's All Done with Mirrors

Practical jokes have much in common with magic. Both are popular art forms based on gulling the innocent, on unexpected surprises, on illusion, and on timing and drama. Also, magicians often have shapely assistants in swimsuits, a fringe benefit which is high on the contract agenda of the Brotherhood of International Practical Jokers, Pranksters, and Yahoos.

Like any good magician, a practical joker will develop and refine his own tricks. He refrains from repeating his past successes before the same audience, for humanity is a fickle creature and is quickly fatigued. Finally, wherever possible, the prankster should keep hidden the means by which the prank was achieved; people love a little mystery, and who are we to deny the innermost cravings of the human heart? Whenever a baffled victim queries "How did you do that?" simply reply "I did it well, of course."

This book contains a description of the choicest practical jokes that I have heard of, have played, or had played on me over the years. Use it wisely, use it well, and use it often. Above all, enjoy yourself now—you only get one chance at life. But one is all you need if you do it right.

"Der Herrgott würfelt nicht"—Albert Einstein
("The Mister God doesn't play dice")

"*. . . aber manchmals spielt er Streiche*"
(". . . but sometimes ze liddle praktikal
jokes, ja hein?")

Tales of the Unexpected

Manhattan.

Early dawn. The city is sleeping. High above the streets, up where only birds can feel truly comfortable, the first light rays of a new day are reaching over pinnacles and spires. Far, far to the east, England is an ocean and a lifetime away. The rain falls lightly as London takes a morning tea break.

But neither of these places has anything at all to do with the subject of this book, so let us leave them alone and concentrate instead on practical jokes. A prankster intent on a practical joke always seeks out the unexpected, the incongruous, the unusual. Do this regularly, and eventually people will come to expect it of you. Fulfilling people's expectations is all very well, but what do you do when people have come to expect the unexpected?

Like Hollywood, underneath all the fake tinsel and glitter, you must give them real tinsel and glitter. Whatever you do, do it to excess, do it in style, and do it to others before they do it to you.

1

I saw my first practical joke at the age of nine years old. A scientifically minded kid brought a reel of thread in to school. For reasons best known to himself, in the morning break he furtively tied the line to a pair of weighing scales on a shelf. He carefully routed the line across the room to his desk, and by tugging it, he could cause the scales to click up and down by remote control.

The next lesson started in the classroom, and the kid

started tugging at the line, slowly at first then more urgently. The scales tapped up and down like a Morse key, and the other kids were very impressed. When the teacher glanced sharply around the room and saw the moving scales, all the kids giggled uncontrollably.

As the teacher walked over to the scales, the kid tugged the line harder and faster. Just as the teacher reached the scales the kid gave the thread a final sharp pull to snap it, thus removing the trail leading to his desk. The scales jumped right off the shelf into the teacher's arms. Kids flew every which way. Kids rolled off desks onto the floor laughing hysterically. Kids staggered to the windows clutching their sides. Kids choked with merriment until stuff ran out of their noses.

I think it is now safe to reveal that I was the kid with the line, and thus was launched a lifetime of arranging humorous surprises.

2

Doors and doorways have so much potential for practical jokers that they deserve a chapter of their own. But they can't have one.

Tie a rubber band, cut from an inner tube, between the inside door handle and something firmly fixed in the room, such as a radiator. Pull the door shut with three strong friends, thus tensioning the rubber band. When the victim opens the door, it catapults inward at great velocity, pulling him with it unless he lets go of the doorknob. I saw this prank played on an obnoxious office worker who always wore a flashy bunch of keys on a chain attached to his pants. He unlocked the door, and it shot inward, jerking the key out of his hand and the pants off his legs.

Apply masking tape over an entire doorframe. This doesn't seem like much, but in order to pass through the victim has to press against all that stickiness (ugh!). A related prank is to paper completely over a door with newspaper or brown paper. This is done on the outward side of an inward-opening door, so that opening the door leaves the paper barrier intact.

Many undergraduates also recommend "empty beer-can barricade" on the outward side of outward-opening doors. Fill the doorway with a carefully, stacked wall of beer cans. Use bedroom doors at night where possible, for the maximum satisfaction from the crashing sound. To obtain the necessary building supplies, simply throw a party.*

While on the subject of door dementia, a perennial favorite is "pennying" someone in, by jamming pennies into a doorframe until it's wedged tight. There are more subtle effects, such as repainting the door during the night or just painting a fancy design on it (say, a shower of golden stars). Engineers can construct and rig a giant palm tree of newspaper to fall in when the door is opened.

3

Take away the moments that make up a dull day with the dummy "broken glass" effect. Use the point of a pin to trace a thin jagged line of Vaseline and sprinkle on some silver glitter. This is effective on a wide range of glass surfaces including windows, mirrors, TVs, computer terminals, spectacles, bottles, vases, drinking glasses, and so on.

The artistic prankster can craft a row of fake bullet holes, say on the bathroom mirror or big sister's car windshield.

Or make a fake broken eyeglass lens: wind black tape around the side pieces, put twenty-three pens and an HP calculator in your shirt pocket; off you go to a costume party, superbly dressed as an "engineering nerd."

---

*See the "Party Time" chapter for more ideas.

4

I always go to meet my friends at the airport when they fly to stay with me. I like to wear a disguise. If they recognize me immediately, then they win. If they can't spot me, even after I walk right over and accost them, then I win. If they approach someone else, and accuse them of being me, then I develop a Freudian identity crisis.

The last time I met my old friend Harris was at the Portland, Oregon, International Airport, and I was posing as a priest. To give Harris a sporting chance, I was also carrying a copy of *Buns 'n Bimbos* magazine under my arm. Before Harris arrived, I was approached by a country bumpkin who wanted to know if I was real. That's a question that a lot of people wonder about, but I assured him that I was, heard his confession, and blessed his livestock.

Another priest also greeted me. How do holy men converse with each other? I nodded back and coughed winsomely, trying to achieve a note of real sincerity and yet regretful apology, that I could not pause to chat. This is a subtle and lengthy nuance to convey in a cough, and I'm not sure the real priest was fully aware of it. But he hurried along. Maybe it was the *Buns 'n Bimbos* that did it.

Other good disguises to adopt: mailman, nun, derelict, pilot, cleaner, punk rocker, Hare Krishna worshipper, businessman, film producer.

5

Fit an acquaintance's car with a slogan license plate holder or bumper sticker. The joke comes in matching the person to the phrase. For example, a slogan reading "Honk if you're horny" or "Too much sex is still not enough" would clearly look good on your grandmother's car. "Born to be hugged" should adorn the car of your greasy cousin Parsnip, while "World's best mother" is more appropriate for grouchy Uncle Kidneybean who forgot your birthday last year. You can change the word *best* to *biggest* if you can find a marker pen.

"Happiness is ballroom dancing" should be fitted to the car of your nineteen-year-old brother, immediately before he drives to meet his gang at the auto-parts store. Grind the peasants into the dirt by tagging some rich old fart's Rolls-Royce with a bumper sticker reading "My other car is a Porsche." Lastly, take the most extravagant, most luxurious car you can find in the corporate parking lot. It is crying out for a bumper sticker sardonically sniveling "For *this* I went to college?"

6

I answered the doorbell one afternoon to find a vaguely familiar man standing on the doorstep with a steaming pizza box in his arms. "Large pizza with extra pepperoni, ten dollars please," he announced. Suddenly I remembered him. He was Roger, the friend of my roommate. We had met briefly at a party months ago. On that occasion he had bounced out of the bathroom, leering an ugly leer full of innuendo and zipping up his fly; he pointed at me and yelled, "Big Bob can manage fun with just one more guy; in you go buddy!" He clapped me on the back and motioned me into the (thankfully empty) bathroom. You've got just two choices with a deep-dish dork like Roger; you can laugh with him or you can laugh at him. A lot of people try to do both at once, and end up choking themselves.

On a whim Roger was now pretending to be a pizza delivery man, instead of my roommate's buddy bringing the football snack. But I remembered his fondness for trickery all too well.

He rolled his eyes and repeated "Extra pepperoni, ten bucks." I grabbed my revenge and the pizza simultaneously. Slamming the door in his face, I thrust ten dollars through the letter box. I had eaten a good half of the pizza before a red-faced Roger managed to get in. It's not often you can boomerang a meathead like Roger the Dodger.

7

I once mailed my brother a stuffed and mounted duck for his birthday. I did this for the confusion factor I knew would result when he unwrapped it. On my next birthday, I received a life-size cardboard skeleton from him. For his next birthday, he got a record of theatrical sound effects from me (complete with the ever-popular "guillotine falling, and head bouncing into basket," and "werewolf devouring victim").

Where can you get a stuffed duck when you need one? I happened to be in Paris at Easter time, where it seems stuffed mounted ducklings and chicks are popular seasonal decorations. Obviously it was too good a chance to miss. I have also seen stuffed ducklings in Germany, in hunting shops. The more practical Teutons employ them as lures or decoys rather than ornamentally as the Gauls do.

Try to extend the idea by visiting a taxidermist, but be sure to find out who really knows his stuff. Procure some really unusual gift: a wolverine, toad, water snake, or sloth, to match the personality of the recipient.

8

One of my favorite pranks is juggling* with uncooked eggs. Women seem strangely ambivalent about this trick. Grab the eggs from their fridge and they really want to see it, but they are not at all keen on having an egg break on the floor. It's exquisite to see them waver

*See prank number 51 for advice on learning to juggle.

between "show me if you can do it" and "you won't make a mess, will you?" I have dropped eggs while practicing this effect in the comfort and privacy of my own home, but none while undertaking a public demonstration. So far.

Use this little prank to make a really big impression on your girlfriend's mother the first time you meet her. Whichever way the trick works out, the mother will remember you for ever.

If you are a chicken (ha-ha!) or not confident of your juggling abilities, secretly substitute eggs that you have previously hard-boiled. If you are expecting someone to pull this stunt on you, then hand them three eggs you have previously "blown" (removed the liquid contents, through a pinhole). It is almost impossible to juggle with such insubstantial eggshells.

9

Switch the labels on two cassettes or records. Cassettes are easier as you just undo the little screws on the case and switch the tape inside. For records, you may have to soak the label off. Don't even think about taking a video tape apart unless you have a degree in engineering, preferably with a major in "teeny little fiddly stuff on springs that flies across the room when you lift the cover off."

This lark produces the best results if you choose tapes with really dissimilar contents, e.g. exchange some classical music and some punk rock. Or arrange matters so that your mother greets her aerobics class with heavy metal instead of jazzercise.

Advanced jokers with access to recording-studio equipment should consider the possibility of using a mixer to slowly fade one type of music into the other. This produces a more subtle and droll effect.

10

My friend Harris was once (and once only) given the job of marking a cross-country racecourse. The trail was to be indicated with red ribbons tied to bushes. Two miles into the course, Harris routed the trail so the runners were brought around in a half-mile circle. The lead runners were aghast when they found that they had rejoined the pack at the rear.

Eventually the competitors picked up the trail again, but Harris had not finished yet. A mile farther on, he rerouted them again so that runners were led into an area of forest plentifully adorned with markers. In fact wherever you stood in a hundred yard radius, you could see a red marker on most points of the compass.

These stratagems delayed the sportsmen long enough to allow Harris to run over the finishing line pushing a baby stroller complete with a portable tape recorder playing sounds of a screaming infant. In front of the Parents' Day audience. A credit to the finest traditions of his school.

11

My list of tools to use in the backyard includes only implements such as the easy chair, sun parasols, iced drinks, and a barbecue grill. To say I don't like gardening is like saying King Herod didn't like children. So it was rather unfortunate when I found myself living in between two horticultural fanatics, who were always trying to encourage me to work in the yard.

I did eventually decide to have a sod lawn laid. When the workmen came, I gave them careful instructions. After the yard had been cleared and the new lawn laid, there in the center remained a large thistle plant. As that chronic smartass Ralph Waldo Emerson once remarked, "A weed is a plant whose virtue has not yet been discovered."

The neighbors were bemused, and confounded. Nurturing the weed became a real project. I secured the thistle to a stake and watered it regularly. Of course, once the plant realized that it was no longer considered unwelcome, it lost its will to live, and died shortly after.

12

When the workmen finished placing the new sod on my lawn, they still had a few squares of surplus turf which they left rolled up by the side of the garden path. The temptation was just too much for Mr. Greenfingers Potato Head next door. Early next morning he jumped over the fence separating our two properties and started busily laying the turf to completely cover up my path. This prank is mild on the amusement scale; a better idea would have been to lay turf over my porch, or to line the walls of my toolshed.

All the while Turnip Brain was chortling a throaty kind of chuckle, and mumbling happily to himself. I let him get as far as the center of my lawn, then turned the sprinkler system on full power. Those who live by the sward shall perish by the sward.

13

One hat I have always wanted for my hat collection is the "propellor hat"—a skull cap with a small spinning propellor blade on top. These were popularized by an elite air-force helicopter unit in Korea in the 1950s and are now rather hard to find. So I was delighted to see a plentiful supply in Disneyland on a recent visit. The staff in the Disneyland shop even embroider your name onto the cap for no extra charge. Naturally, for a kid's cap like this you should have a really tough name put on it. I considered "Rambo," "Killer," "Hulk," etc., before finally settling on "Knuckles."

As I came up to the Disneyland ticket office, I was pleased to see that the admission price is reduced for ministers wearing their clerical garb. I was particularly pleased since I had my priest's collar with me in the car. I never travel far without it, on the "physician, heal thyself" principle. Also, clerical garb is of great assistance in getting better odds when trying to hustle pool in small towns. In certain parts of Wyoming, they probably still talk in hushed tones about the preacher of the pool halls who drifted into town one night and cleaned them all out.

14

I once shared an old house with Harris, and the experience has proved a rich source of practical jokes. Like the time it rained solidly for three days. The roof in my bedroom started to leak, so I placed a bucket underneath the drip and went to tell the landlord. "The rain is coming through my ceiling. How long is this going to last?" I complained. "What do you think I am," growled the tetchy landlord in response, "a weather prophet?"

Eventually he agreed to take a look at the problem. The landlord and I returned to the house together. Everything was as before, except that there was now a goldfish swimming happily in the bucket of rainwater under the roof leak.

I still don't know how Harris thought of the idea, obtained a goldfish, and installed it during the brief time I was gone. He doesn't move that quickly nowadays.

15

Never miss the opportunity to show off in a foreign language. If someone asks you to tell a joke, always give them one in French, German, or Russian. My German dictionary lists the English translation of the German word *Weltanschauung* as "Weltanschauung."* Now that's a degree of accuracy on which you can rely. It certainly captures every nuance of the word in its German form. There is no way to be sure if this is a proofreader's inadvertent slip or a deliberate prank played on readers. But we can always hope.

Actually, there do seem to be differences in patterns of national humor. For example, the following are typical French jokes. Memorize them, and when the boys are huddled around the bar, knocking back the firewater and swapping stories, let them have it in French.

Quelle différence y a-t-il entre un bouchon de champagne et un enfant?

Réponse: le bouchon de champagne porte à coup sûr le nom du fabricant.

"Maman," questionne une petit fille de dix ans, "est-ce que je peux avoir des enfants?" "Bien sûr que non," fait sa mère en riant. "Youpee!" hurle la gamine. Et se précipitant dehors pour rejoindre trois garnements plus âgés qu'elle: "Allez les gars, on recommence."

Dans la cour de l'école, deux gamines, très fières l'une et l'autre, rivalisent d'érudition: "Moi, dit la première, je sais comment on fait les bébés." "Peuh!" s'écrie la seconde, "c'est simpliste. Mais moi, je sais comment on ne les fait pas."

Aux États-Unis, dans la plupart des chambres d'hôtels, une Bible est à la disposition des voyageurs. Un jour, un client de passage trouve cette note dans le Livre

---

*"Weltanschauung" is actually a philosophical term meaning "an outlook, or perspective, on the world," as in "Because he was such a sawn-off little runt, Toulouse Lautrec had a real low-life Weltanschauung."

saint, posé sur la table de nuit: "Si vous êtes seul et triste, cherchez le réconfort en lisant les psaumes 23, 25, 27."

En dessous, une main anonyme avait ajouté: "Et si vous n'êtes pas consolé après cela, téléphonez au 91-54-85. Demandez qu'on vous passe Barbara."

The English translations are:

Q. What is the difference between a champagne cork and a baby?
A. The champagne cork always bears the definite name of the maker.

"Mother," asked a little ten-year-old girl, "am I able to have babies?" "Of course not," replied her mother, laughing. "Aw-*right!*" cheered the girl. And running outside to rejoin three older rascals, she exclaimed, "C'mon boys, let's get back to it!"

A young boy runs into a police station and calls for help because his father is in a brawl outside. The sergeant goes outside with the lad where two men are fighting on the sidewalk. "Which one is your dad?" demands the policeman. "That's what they're fighting about," shoots back the kid.

In a World War II prisoner of war camp, a new prisoner arrives and attends his first camp entertainment meeting. An officer is on stage reading out numbers, "23, 25, 27," each of which is greeted with hilarious laughter. Seeing the bewilderment of the new prisoner, an old hand explains that the camp has so many old jokes that to save energy they assigned them all a number and merely call out the number instead of telling the whole joke.

The new prisoner thinks this is a great idea and tries it for himself. "91-54-85," he calls out to prolonged and uproarious laughter. "Very good indeed," compliments the old sweat, "we hadn't heard those before."

Trés drôle, but if you wake up in the middle of the night to find your bed shaking with laughter, check for indigestion first.

16

One ploy that can be used to make fun of almost any picture is the Devise-a-Slogan competition. Simply place a plain piece of paper underneath the offending poster and invite people to write their own captions to the picture. Start them off with a few entries of your own to get the ball rolling.

The slogans that people think of will either be very funny or total rubbish. My town newspaper recently ran a slogan competition with a picture of a local collapsed bridge. The winning caption was "And the good news is: toll charges have also been dropped." Fifty-seven other people submitted the slogan "Oops!" Could these dunces really think that caption was in the least bit witty? Taken in aggregate, these entrants obviously had a total IQ approaching that of a sand lizard.

17

Remember always that the essence of a practical joke is to deal up the unexpected, and this can be done in the simplest of ways. I used to live about ten yards from a really good restaurant, which enabled me to set up a friend of mine visiting from out of town.

One evening I suggested eating out, and we got into my car. I drove us all over town for about twenty minutes to fix the impression that we were traveling a long way, then secretly circled back to the restaurant, which was actually just seconds from my front door.

Inside we had the usual good time, lubricated by good food and fine wine. When we were finished, I pointed out it would be foolhardy to drive with this level of blood in the alcoholstream and suggested that we enjoy the fine night by walking home. My friend agreed and we set out on the "long" walk home. Almost immediately I stopped at a front door and turned my key in the lock. Collapse of stout party.

Variant: A year later, I was living in a condominium with a swimming pool, and caught the same friend with this trick in reverse. Proposing a swimming trip, I loaded the car with the towels and swimsuits, checked the oil, fuel, and tires, got everybody in the car, and then finally . . . drove seven yards across the lot to the pool. The pool wasn't previously visible, for it lay behind a waist-high wooden fence. It's hard to maintain a straight face when announcing arrival two seconds after departure.

18

A high-school student entered a nationwide contest hoping to win a new car. His coworkers at the local burger joint knew someone who was traveling to Florida, where the contest was organized. They typed up an official-looking letter, and had it mailed from Florida, notifying the dupe that he had won the fabulous new car.

So far, a standard "spoof letter" prank. But the zinger that makes the hoax even better is that the duped student had a nosy mother who opened his mail and duly found the fake prize notification. She went directly to the local high school and hauled her son out of class to tell him that he had won the car. Later that day when the truth was known, the angry mother visited the homes of each of the conspirators and screamed and yelled at them, their parents, relatives, ancestors, pets, and so on.

The next day these same conspirators bet her son that he could not chew a whole box of Chicklets gum. The poor innocent won the bet, not knowing that his coworkers had substituted a laxative gum of identical appearance. He did find out later, though.

19

Many houses and apartments have a cold-water tank, usually somewhere overhead. This tank holds the cold-water supply for the dwelling and is replenished from the water main. The tank tends to lie undisturbed for years at a time, and often accumulates a harmless brown sediment at the bottom.

If you sharply tap the base of the tank, it will stir up some of this detritus, and the water in the house will run brown for a couple of hours. If you really want to get a name for being a nuisance, you could add a few drops of food coloring to the water supply. Variety, as always, is the name of the game here. Make the water run red, white, and blue over successive hours on patriotic holidays.

Classical
Pranks

Some practical jokes have been around for years and are well known to a large audience. These pranks are the humorous equivalent of bottles of aged wine. You guessed it; they are dull, stale, and cracked.

Other practical jokes have become a part of popular urban mythology, along with other twentieth-century legends such as the machete-wielding little-old-lady hitch-hiker and discarded pet crocodiles breeding in city sewers.

The older and more famous classical pranks are mostly complete rubbish. Many of the newer ones are worth aspiring to. They are all described here, so judge for yourself which is which.

20

Since time immemorial, pranksters have been planting hoax exhibits in museums. One of the cleverest is the fake "Van Gogh ear." Van Gogh, it will be recalled, was the whacky Dutch impressionist painter who chopped off his ear. Some claim it was to express contrition after a fist fight with Gauguin. Others say it was to send to his French mistress. I think that he hoped she would whisper sweet nothings into it, whether he was there or not.

The dummy-ear hoax was created in 1935 by the American prankster Hugh Troy. He crafted a dummy ear from wax and infiltrated it into the Museum of Modern Art in New York during a Van Gogh exhibition. Identified by a label, and placed in a velvet-lined box on a collapsible plinth, the ear drew as much interest and admiration as the paintings.

The Metropolitan Museum of Art held a major Van Gogh exhibition in January 1987, which I attended in eager anticipation of seeing more and greater hoax exhibits of Van Gogh appendages; but all I got was a big fat nothing. New York ain't what it used to be, if it ever was.

The stunt can be carried to ludicrous extremes. For example, smuggle a human cranium (or replica) into a museum exhibition case and mark it "Napoleon's skull." Place a much smaller cranium next to it marked "Napoleon's skull when a boy."

21

Every modern book of puzzles includes the "joke that doesn't come" conundrum. It's usually described in terms of an older brother promising his sibling that he'll trick him with a good prank the next day. Accordingly the young fellow is doubly alert all day long, but agonizes because he can detect nothing amiss. At the very end of the day, the elder brother confesses that his prank was . . . to not play a prank.

Has the younger brother been tricked or not? He didn't get something he expected, and on those grounds some people agree that he has been fooled. However, other people argue that being fooled is "*actually* getting something that you did not expect" rather than "*not* getting something you did expect," hence the boy hasn't been fooled.

My answer is: save the double crosses, triple bluffs, and other semantic foreplay for the CIA. The only person getting suckered by the analysis of prank philosophy is the reader trying to follow it all. Don't worry about it, and don't waste your time with puzzle books when you could waste your time much more effectively with this practical-joke book.

22

There are two stations on the London Underground (subway system) that are both called "Edgeware Road." They are on opposite sides of the Marylebone Flyover (overpass). They connect to different lines. This is bad, since they don't connect underground, but at least they are near enough to be thought of as the same station.

But worse than this, there are two completely different subway stations, about half a mile apart, both called "Shepherd's Bush." It turns out that these stations date from pre-1930 when there were many different railway companies operating in London. One of the Shepherd's Bushes* was built and operated by the Central London Railway, while the other served the Great Western and Hammersmith Railway.

In 1930 the London Transport Board was created to amalgamate public transport in the capital, and so inherited multiple stations bearing the same name. Both stations are in the general Shepherd's Bush vicinity (albeit at opposite ends of it) and the fare is the same from either place. It's less trouble to put up with two identically named stations than it is to try to change one of them, so the situation persists to this day. It's a bit tough on strangers, though.

If you are ever in London and have to meet someone you'd prefer to avoid, then arrange the rendezvous for "Shepherd's Bush tube station ticket office."

23

Some evergreen practical jokes wax and wane in popularity but never disappear completely. A few years ago

---

*Quick test on the rules of English grammar: If the plural of "court-martial" is "courts-martial" and the plural of "trade union" is "trades unions," should the plural of "banana split" be "bananas split"? And what is the plural of "Shepherd's Bush"? Should Shepherds be allowed more than one bush each?

it seemed as though every mail box in town had been candy-striped. Some joker was going around with a can of white paint, diligently applying this artistic improvement. I wouldn't recommend this because the authorities take a dim view of free-lance efforts to upgrade their chosen color scheme. But on the other hand, it doesn't hurt anyone, and it's all the same to me what color mailbox I mail my letters in.

Right now, the white paint prank-of-the-moment seems to be the "murder-victim outline," which is applied in various places for maximum effect: on city hall steps, outside art galleries, on garage doors, and (maximum bonus points for effort) on the ceiling over an office stairwell.

24

Then there is the ever-popular fake letter. No special effort is taken to make it too authentic. If realism is a must, then you could photocopy one from this book. It is normally typed on plain paper and mailed to the victim. It is polite to refer to the letter in conversation with your victim afterward so he will know who to thank.

One fake letter purports to inform the recipient that his "optrectomy" operation has been scheduled. It runs something like this:

Dear Mr. Flatulent,

This letter is to inform you that your optrectomy operation has been arranged for next Tuesday at 2:30 P.M. As you may be aware this is a delicate surgical procedure that will sever the nerve connecting your rectum to your eyeball, and hopefully it will cure your shitty outlook on life.

Yours sincerely,

Cityville Medical Services

Another classic letter appears to be from a minister who travels around the country lecturing on the evils of drink:

Dear Mr. Flatulent,

Please allow me to introduce myself as the Reverend Archibald Parsifal. My life is dedicated to touring the country giving public lectures on the evils of alcohol. I find myself in need of some help, and some mutual friends have suggested that you might be able to aid me.

I have been accompanied on my travels by an assistant, Basil. Basil is an unfortunate creature, totally addicted to strong liquor. He appears on stage with me: frail, drooling, and demented, a pitiful example of where drinking inevitably leads. Many young people have been converted to abstinence after seeing Basil.

Unfortunately Basil recently died, and friends who know you well have put your name forward as his replacement. If you would be interested in this post, please could you reply as soon as possible as I am anxious to get to work before you become too weak to travel.

Yours sincerely,

Rev. Archibald Parsifal

The most insidious letter is simply the following typed on a plain sheet of white paper. The best pranks are often the least complicated.

The police are watching you.
Act normal.

It is said that a hoaxer once telegrammed this message to every member of the British Houses of Parliament, and six of them immediately took flight.

I receive at least one of these fake letters every six months or so. If I go through half a year and still haven't got one, I call all my friends to comment on the fact. That usually brings a selection by the next mail.

25

A time-honored office gag centers around the pompous manager who makes a big show of his importance. This sort of person invariably lugs an impressive briefcase into work every day. Although he never reveals the contents, the briefcase actually contains nothing more important than his lunchtime sandwiches. The prank is to pad the case with a slim but heavy object. A foot-square pane of thick glass works well. You can slip it unobtrusively behind the document compartment. The chances are he'll be carrying it around for weeks.

If he does find it prematurely, he'll probably puzzle for the rest of his life over where it came from and why. Or if he fingers you as the culprit and demands an explanation, just shrug your shoulders and tell him, "No pane, no gain."

That snappy phrase was coined in a speech by Adlai Stevenson accepting the presidential nomination in July 1952 at an oceanside convention. Which just goes to show you can lead a Norse to water, but you can't make him think.

26

Have you ever gone to what you thought would be a great movie, only to find that the best part was the closing credits? This experience inspired my colleague Larry to create a classic technological prank: jamming the audio at a drive-in movie and inserting a new and different sound track.

Larry was in his second year of electrical engineering at college, and had both the time and the knowledge to devote to several weeks of skillful preparation. He scrounged an old but powerful public-address-system amplifier and modified it to run from an external DC power supply provided by an army-surplus dynamotor. The dynamotor in turn was powered by a temporary installation of two car batteries. The whole assembly was put in the trunk of a car. A reconnaissance at the target drive-in indicated that a seventy-volt transformer was mounted in the base of each speaker pedestal. It would be easy to backfeed into the system.

On the fateful night, Larry and two carloads of supporters infiltrated the drive-in. They parked in the last row. Under cover of darkness, they removed the cover at the base of the speaker pedestal and attached two magnetic wires to the seventy-volt feed. Luckily there was enough clearance to allow the wires to pass through when the cover was replaced. The magnetic connections allowed for a rapid and inconspicuous breakaway.

The feature movie was a low-budget horror film about witches and the supernatural, perfect for a "commentary." With all connections made, Larry turned on the dynamotor. The vacuum tubes warmed up, and he cautiously advanced the master gain control. Success!

Larry and the supporters then overdubbed a running commentary that is perhaps best left to the imagination (e.g., film showed an evil witch screaming and cackling; the fake voice-over had her saying, "A mouse! A mouse just ran up my broomstick!"). The audience went wild: people were falling about with laughter, blowing their car horns, catcalling and whistling in delight. The drive-in management went bananas.

After a few minutes, two people ran out of the projection booth with flashlights and started checking cars. It was time to pull the plug. The usher who came over to Larry's car viewed it with great suspicion, since he and the people in the two adjacent support cars were still laughing hysterically. However, no one said anything—the drive-in management was probably in a state of shock that someone had the capability to wage such electronic warfare.

27

Secretly place a couple of very thin slices of carrot into a goldfish tank. Later when you have an audience, snatch the slices out and eat them. If you are fast enough, people will assume that you are gobbling the fish.

Your eyesight has to be good for this one, otherwise you could find yourself really chewing sushi. If this does happen, a sense of loyalty to other pranksters would demand that you swallow it anyway. Or you could do what Harris did: throw it back, complaining that it was "too small."

28

For as long as there have been soldiers, there have been other soldiers nailing their boots to the floor. At any time archaeologists could unearth a fragment of Roman mosaic reading "*Salve Brute! Crepidas meas per clavos ad solum adfixitne?*"*

Barracks floors are often bare wooden boards, and soldiers always leave their boots by the bedside at night. These two factors interact by an unwritten law of nature, as strong as the law of nature governing "the further away you have to park, the more empty parking places you pass walking in from your car."

Normally the victim with the immobilized footwear starts to get dressed in the morning but discovers he cannot move his boots from where they stand. He tries to pull the nails out with his teeth but eventually has to go on parade in his carpet slippers.

It would be a real zinger to secure the boots to the floor while the occupant is still in them. Nailing boots to the floor definitely ruins the footwear, and usually the floor, too. For a less destructive variant, try to wire them to the floor instead, using the lace holes.

*"Hey Brutus! Did you nail my sandals to the floor?"

29

"It's a very eerie feeling, to read your own obituary" was how the noted humorist Alan Abel of Connecticut described the results of his greatest hoax. Alan wanted to see if it was possible to get his obituary published in the *New York Times*, and he devoted his considerable talents to the project. And of course, there are also substantial tax advantages for taxpayers who can arrange to be dead one year in every three, on a regular basis.

A fake funeral home was set up in Orem, Utah, and a telephone installed. Alan booked into Robert Redford's Sundance Ski Lodge and stayed overnight before staging a "tragic accident" on a ski trail the next day. A fake funeral director from the fake funeral home later turned up at the lodge to collect Alan's effects, and the project was under way.

An actress friend posed as Alan's grieving widow, and the story was fed to the *Times* on New Year's Day 1980, when most of the regular journalists were at home nursing hangovers. Even so, the *New York Times* was impressively thorough in its checking. The obituary writer telephoned the ski lodge, the fake funeral home, and the church that was booked for the wake. Alan's careful planning paid off, and despite his reputation as a prankster, the obituary was printed.

As Woody Allen put it, "I don't want to achieve immortality through my work. I want to achieve immortality through not dying." The obituary of the man who invented the six-pack of beer appeared the same day as Alan's. He only rated three paragraphs. Alan got six. I would say that Alan had achieved Woody's goal.

30

In turn-of-the-century England, back when General Electric was still only a Major, the so-called Bloomsbury set were the literary lions of the cultural menagerie.

Dominated by Virginia Woolf, they wrote a lot of dull prose, but in February 1910 managed to pull off a practical joke. Virginia, her brother, and three or four other cronies dressed up as—get this—the Emperor of Abyssinia and retinue, to make an official visit to the battleship HMS *Dreadnought*. They persuaded a friend in the Foreign Office to send a telegram scheduling the visit. They then took the train to Weymouth and were duly given the brief reception on board that the government had requested.

Talk about tedious; this hardly qualifies as a hoax at all. They were announced through official channels, and furthermore the vessel's commander was a cousin of Virginia and her brother, hence they were moving in totally familiar circles and were in no danger of being clapped in irons or keel-hauled or forced to serve under Al Haig or anything. In later years, Virginia was said to render audiences "helpless with laughter" by telling this tale. Maybe she did good impressions or something. Classical practical jokes have come a long way since 1910.

31

In the past few years the *Guardian* newspaper in England has been running its own April 1 practical jokes. In 1986, this extended to some of the advertising. The paper carried a half-page BMW ad describing the virtues of their latest car-safety feature. Complete with a cutaway engineering diagram, the ad described a mechanism that allowed you to raise or lower tire pressures while driving along. It had me fooled.

The *Guardian* started this modern tradition on April 1, 1977, with a long travel supplement on the (totally fictitious) country of San Seriffe. There was no way of telling the spoof article from the real thing, since it was every bit as boring and pointless as a genuine travel supplement. Rather a lot of the place names in San

Seriffe were also printer's terms, (such as Em, Bodoni, and Pica), but most of these names are about as meaningful to the general public as the instructions that come with a Japanese camera.

Other newspapers have since climbed on the bandwagon. In 1985, the London *Sunday Times* had a front-page story giving details of the test transmission of a new pirate TV pornography channel. While I was breathlessly adjusting the TV tuner, my brother (with the stuffed duck, see ruse number 7) gleefully pointed out the proximity of the date to April 1. You *can* fool all of the people all of the time: just tell them what they want to hear.

Apocryphal
Anecdotes

Practical jokes are based on the unexpected. And what could be more unexpected than the frankly incredible? These fairy tales are too good to leave out. Some of them might even be true.

Everyone knows someone whose cousin's brother met someone else on a plane, who says it almost happened, in a modified form, to a friend of his. There are certain similarities running through many of these apocryphal antics. One concludes that the ultimate apocryphal joke would be the result of a bet, made between an undergraduate and a celebrity, on Parents' Day, and would involve an animal. I still don't believe a word of any of them.

32

They say that salesmen are the easiest people to sell, and perhaps comedians are the easiest people to make fun of. The TV host Johnny Carson supposedly arranged a surprise for comedienne Joan Rivers. In her act Joan is often outspoken, particularly about Britain and the British royal family. Carson noticed this, and hired an actress to impersonate the first lady of British royalty, namely Prime Minister Margaret Thatcher.

When Joan arrived at the Los Angeles airport to appear on Carson's show, Carson staged an "accidental" meeting between Joan and the Maggie impostor. This was a cleverly thought-out plan, because it is quite plausible that the Premier would be passing through the airport.

The Maggie imposter then "recognized" Joan Rivers and started to berate her, complaining about her anti-British and anti-Royal jokes. Poor Joan was completely taken in, apologized, and promised to mend her ways. The whole scene was recorded by Johnny's hidden cameras.

Come on, now! Get real! Maybe it happened, but was Joan really completely unaware of the prank, and not in on the joke? She earns her living by being professionally humorous, and she does a better job when she has the opportunity to rehearse.

33

The medieval English politician Sir Thomas More once commented on the ease with which he could translate into Latin and Greek. A friend wagered that he could not translate any arbitrary verse. Sir Thomas accepted the bet, and as a prank the friend gave him, not some classical verse, but the popular medieval limerick:

> There was a young man of Devizes
> Whose ears were of different sizes
> One was so small,
> It was nothing at all,
> While the other won several prizes.

More thought about this for a short time and produced the stunningly accurate Latin rendition:

> *Erat incola Divisarum*
> *Dispar modus auricularum*
> *Una haec nihili,*
> *Palma triplici,*
> *Iam erat altera claram*

*How many stupid little footnotes can you get in a book?

"But what," inquired the wagering well-wisher, "of the Greek translation?" Obligingly, More then went on to produce . . . but no! The Latin verse alone is surely worth the price of this book. The Greek translation is left as an exercise to the reader. If the reader needs still more exercise, then do twenty-five push-ups followed by twenty-five sit-ups. In my case this would probably be followed by twenty-five throwing-ups.

34

A disgruntled group of graduating high-school students in an agricultural region are said to have hired a crane, lifted a cow from an adjacent field, and lowered it into the school courtyard. When the cow was discovered the next morning, it proved to be too wide to take out through any of the doorways.

The cow had to remain there for several weeks until the same crane could be rehired to lift it out again. In the meantime it had to be milked, fed, and cleaned up everyday.

35

The story is told of the rivalry between Bob Hope and Bing Crosby. Between engagements, they visited the Santa Anita Racetrack, where Bob wagered that he could pick more winners during the day than Bing. Naturally the old crooner accepted the bet speedily, confident that he was much more knowledgeable about horseflesh than Hope was. Then Bing began to wonder if Bob was planning some kind of trick, for he knew nothing about horses. To protect himself Bing made a plan of his own.

Before each race the cocky comedians would go to different betting windows and pick their horse. At the end of the first race, they both produced a winning ticket. When the second race was run, again each showed the other a betting receipt naming the winning animal. After the third race, they both had winners for the third time! And the lucky streak continued for both of them in exactly this way for the whole afternoon's racing.

Their wager with each other was a draw, but on the way home Crosby asked Hope how he got so lucky. "I thought I'd take you, Pappy," was Hope's easy response, "but you got too lucky. I bought a two-dollar ticket on *every* horse in each race, so I couldn't lose!"

It was Bing's turn to laugh, and he made it a side-splitter. "I figured you were pulling some kind of trick on me. So not to be outsmarted, I did exactly the same thing myself!"

36

An old standby, popular in offices is the "hat of varying sizes." Your victim must be someone who habitually wears the same hat. You secretly find out his hat size and buy two others of the exact type, one slightly larger and one slightly smaller. By adroit substitution over a period of weeks you can make him believe his head is growing and shrinking periodically.

The basic scheme can be applied to many different objects. The "growing-and-shrinking pet tortoise" is the best known. This variant was supposedly played by a professor who had the apartment above an old lady. This old lady kept a pet tortoise on the balcony. She had crossed the professor in some way, and he took advantage of the fact that his balcony overlooked hers. Every day he would lower a new, slightly larger tortoise on a rope, and snag up the old one. When the apparent growth in the pet was so large that the old lady called the zoo, the professor reversed the process for an even more astonishing effect.

*before anyone notices them?

History does not relate what the professor did with his twenty assorted tortoises when the prank was over. Personally, I don't believe a word of it. Just as any dirty joke is enhanced 20 percent when a bishop features in it (63.8 percent if an actress appears, too), so any practical joke gains 20 percent when a professor is involved.

I'd recommend that you try this trick with horticulture instead. Imagine the consternation when a gardener notices that his blooms seem to be reversing the normal growing process, gradually turning from large plants back into seedlings. Marigolds are very good for this prank. They are cheap, widely available, have a long growing season, and are colorful enough to be noticed. The final zinger, when you have shrunk the plants down to tiny seedlings, is to remove them altogether and leave packets of seeds in their place.

37

The English word *quiz* is reputed to be a neologism, the result of a bet in Victorian England to put this made up word on the lips of all London. The man who wagered that he could do this simply painted the word on walls all over London. Sure enough, within a month, all London was commenting on the strange new graffito, and the bet was won.

My Concise Oxford dictionary indeed lists the derivation of *quiz* as "nineteenth-century dialect of unknown origin." My own theory is that *quiz* is no more than a contraction or corruption of the word *inquisition*. Of course it might be that this interesting derivation story was itself put about as a prank, particularly because the original usage of quiz referred to a yo-yo.

38

The Europeans have a type of pear liqueur that comes in a fat bottle with a narrow neck. The bottle contains a real whole pear, bobbing around in the liqueur. The way they get the pear in the bottle is to grow it in there, by slipping the bottle over a bud in spring. The orchards look a sight with thousands of bottles strapped onto tree branches. On the same principle you could secretly rear a creature, say a hippo, in your mother's boudoir, until it was full size, and too large to remove without dismantling the house. The only difficulty (and it is probably why nobody has done this yet) would be keeping it hidden for three years until the dénouement of the exercise.

A whole class of apocryphal pranks is concerned with secretly smuggling animals, usually barnyard animals, into places where they would not usually be found. For example, the stories are told of the horse in the dean's study, the pig in the girls' dorm, the bull in the china shop, the dog in the manger, the fly in the ointment, the twinkle in your eye, and so on ad nauseam.

In general, the organization required to stage animal pranks, when compared with the mild laugh payoff, makes them suitable mostly for bank clerks who don't know any better. Not that I have anything against bank clerks, but if they are so good at counting, why do they always have eight windows but only four tellers?

39

In a certain university which shall remain nameless (but which is actually the University of Connecticut at Storrs, near Hartford) it was the weekend for parents to visit the institution.

An enterprising engineering student gathered all of the empty Coke crates from around campus and brought them back to his dormitory. He then used the crates to build a whole series of new internal walls in the building. He papered over the crates with brown wrapping paper stolen from somewhere else on campus, making substantial and realistic partitions.

The new layout of the dormitory ensured that people

on the third floor had to go down to the second floor to find a bathroom, people on the second floor had to go up to the third floor, while people on the fifth floor had to descend to the fourth floor. And so on for all seven floors of the dormitory. Since it was Parents' Weekend all the freshmen had their parents in tow, so nobody felt like acting outrageously and kicking down the barricades.

The unknown student constructor, class of 1969, surely deserved a special prize for "extramural activities."

40

The *Alice in Wonderland* and *Through the Looking Glass* stories of Lewis Carroll are two of the most popular books of the Victorian era, rivaling even Dickens in appeal. "Lewis Carroll" was merely a nom de plume adopted by the logician Charles L. Dodgson, to keep private his true profession as a lecturer in mathematics at Oxford University. And knowing the way most university professors live, who could blame him?

The great Queen Victoria herself is said to have read the *Alice* books and enjoyed them very much. The story goes that she then commanded all other writing by the same author to be brought to her. Royal equerries hurried to fulfill her wish, and soon collected the complete published works of Dodgson. Apart from the *Alice* books, this consisted entirely of complex mathematical papers, technical treatises, and books† on symbolic logic.

*Lots, I'll bet.

†One of Dodgson's books, *A Tangled Tale*, is a collection of recreational mathematical problems that includes the following delightful rhyme as a chapter heading:

"*One piecee thing that my have got,
Maskee‡ that thing my no can do.
You talkee you no sabey what ?
    Bamboo.*"

‡"*Maskee*" in Pidgin English means "without," if that's any help in deciphering this lilting lyric. Forget about big-eared freaks from Devizes; this is the rhyme I would challenge Sir Thomas More to translate into Latin and Greek (see prank 33).

These were humbly laid before the queen, while the royal courtiers stifled hysterical giggles in the background. The reaction of the matronly old monarch is unrecorded, but it is probably safe to assume this was another one of the occasions when she was "not amused."

The Joy
of Junk

The very best practical jokes don't need any artificial dissemination. But there are many acceptable pranks that do use some equipment. I give the name *junk jokes* to pranks that rely on some special gimmick apparatus, or where the equipment is the joke.

Over the years I have amassed a large collection of fun stuff. Looking quickly around my house, I can see: a rubber duck (not a bathtub toy, but a rubber plucked duck), a lifesize cardboard skeleton, an inflatable great white shark (suitable for dressing in a pair of sunglasses and a beach hat, and leaving in the shower stall at parties), a swimming toy hippo (for livening up your partner's bathtub fun), a whoopee cushion that makes a farting sound when depressed (don't we all?), a six-foot-high inflatable Godzilla (also looks good in a T-shirt at parties), a set of false teeth (it's surprisingly hard to ventriloquize with these), a Groucho Marx false mustache and glasses (usually being worn on the bill of the rubber duck), a rubber cockroach, a pirate hat (wear this on board any boat you command), a pirate flag (postcard size, for the boat or a car aerial), a squashed-face rubber ball, a mechanical toy monkey that plays the cymbals, and much more besides.

One item I don't have, but which I've always coveted, is a realistic-looking pistol that ejects a flag from the barrel when fired, reading "BANG." I always ask for this when I visit a joke shop, but so far with no result. The one thing that keeps me going is the idea of depreciating all this junk on my tax return, if I ever earn a living as a consultant practical joker.

41

My "Zany Zappers" are one of the most prized assets of the junk-joke collection. These are a pair of dark glasses that light up with a red light in the center of each lens when a concealed hand switch is pressed. Operated in the dark, Zany Zappers give the wearer a diabolic appearance. I gave my Zany Zappers their first trial at a nighttime open-air Christmas Eve carol service. Singing lustily, I tapped the hand switch in time to the rhythm. The effect was everything I hoped for, so much so that the vicar lost his place in the songbook, one nervous old woman fainted, and a church warden asked me to leave.

42

At college I put together a fake thesis. It has the exact appearance of a Master of Science dissertation, but every sentence in the body is randomly generated by computer. It took me about an hour to supply the vocabulary and grammar from which it was generated, and a further day to write the abstract, introduction, and index, to print it out, and get it bound. I entitled it *Computerized Dissertation Synthesis*, and I still keep a copy on a bookshelf at home. It contains wholly meaningless, yet strangely powerful and deep passages, like:

The implementation of instructions in the conditional category promotes efficient utilization of the hardware provided by the design in the main processor and the coprocessor. The condition on which the instruction execution is based is related to the coprocessor operation and is therefore evaluated by the coprocessor. The instruction completion following the condition evaluation is, however, directly related to the operation of the main processor. And a buffer will cycle the bandwidth.

People browsing through my library often pick it up, and it's entertaining to see how quickly they realize it is bogus. Some people never do catch on that it's a joke ("It's about computers, right? So I don't expect to understand one word of it anyway"). Regrettably, I never managed to infiltrate a copy into the Sterling Memorial Library or the Beinecke Rare Book Library at Yale.

There seems to be a wave of bogus books. While browsing through the excellent Parnassus Bookstore on Massachusetts's Cape Cod, I found a slim volume in the "Crime" section entitled *How to Hold Up A Bank*. It turned out to be a treatise on preventing soil erosion on embankments on Long Island. Naturally, I bought it at once. I keep it next to my 1899 edition of Charles Darwin's *Insectivorous Plants*. My local bookstore recently featured a book called *The Ethics of Wall Street*. Somehow you just knew it was going to be totally blank without even opening it.

Finally, no matter what the subject of a book, it's a valuable marketing aid to print "How to become FABULOUSLY RICH" prominently on the cover. This appeals directly to the warmest instinct of the American heart. Exactly: greed.

43

My friend Harris's birthday was coming up, and he had been constantly talking about his desire for a birthday cake for the past four weeks. Obviously some kind of stunt was essential, but what exactly? My vote was to try to procure one of those banquet cakes from which a dancer bursts.

I had been curious about these for some time (the cakes, not the dancers). What was it like inside the cake: was it dark or could the occupant pass the time by reading? Could the occupant breathe fresh air, and was there a comfortable place to sit? One thing was certain, the dancer need never be hungry: not while surrounded by all that cake.

The dancer-in-the-cake stunt was reluctantly dropped for lack of time and money. And now a quick fast cheap gag was needed more than ever. The local joke shop saved the day with a box of "never die" candles. These amazing little candles can't be blown out. They really can't. You can extinguish them momentarily, but the flame comes right back. I don't know how these work; maybe Jehovah's Witnesses make them.

44

Paste your picture in a pinup book and leave it around for your loved ones. The junk-book section in my supermarket recently had a book titled *The 30 Most Eligible Bachelors*. Furthermore *Cosmopolitan* magazine regularly publishes a "Bachelor of the Month" story. Either of these would be suitable. They usually feature some overbronzed jock lawyer, so use the opportunity to redress the balance in favor of starch-haired pencil-necked geeks, e.g.:

(your name), heir to a vast hemorrhoid-ointment fortune, is pictured here indulging two of his favorite pastimes: watching football and drinking beer. "I guess I've always liked beer," confesses a smiling (your name), "ever since I accidentally fell in a vat of dad's home brew at an early age. Since I can't swim, I almost drowned, and had to climb out of the vat three times to take a leak." (your name) is also fond of staring aimlessly into space, claiming it helps him relax and get ready for another arduous day reading trust-fund reports on the increase in his net worth.

(your name) is actively searching for his ideal soulmate, mostly by studying cheerleader rehearsals through binoculars. "I have a pretty good idea of what my future partner is like," says soft-voiced (your name). "She's intelligent, knowledgeable on current affairs, decisive, independent, and she'll probably be wearing a black leather mini-skirt, high-heeled shoes, and one of those tiny see-through halter tops with the low-cut front. She almost certainly lives in a penthouse on top of a bar, overlooking a premier league football stadium somewhere."

(your name) is prepared to compromise on all of the above, except the black leather miniskirt.

To meet interesting new friends you could try placing a similarly worded ad in the Personals column of any large city newspaper, and see what turns up. Be careful here; I once advertised in a newspaper for a saxophone instructor and got phone calls from every pervert in town. Yes, the word *saxophone* was spelt out in full in the ad. There must either be some kind of weird subliminal image associated with the instrument, or else I inadvertently stumbled on some degenerate code phrase.

45

My brother gave me a lifesize three-dimensional cardboard skeleton for my birthday. It was a novel and delightful gift, and I assembled it over the next few weeks. It was made from folding stiff cardboard and held together by paper fasteners. I spread it out on the living-room floor and idly experimented with repositioning the limbs (hang the left leg off a shoulder joint, connect the right arm to the neck, bolt the head onto the wrist of the right arm, etc.) I had just succeeded in assembling an extraordinary crablike creature when the doorbell rang. It was the local vicar. I left him in the hall, but he kept darting nervous glances over my shoulder at the monstrous pile of bones. He only stayed a few seconds before backing out. What a pity I didn't have the Zany Zappers handy.

Since then, Windy the skeleton has put in a full tour of duty. I take him to work once a year or so. Naturally he travels in the front passenger seat wearing a seat belt. At work, I generally set him up at somebody's desk, hunched over a computer terminal.

At home, I had great plans for storing Windy inside the cabinet of my grandfather clock, but he is slightly too large. So he has to stay in a closet, large cupboard, or refrigerator. An arm is easily pinned so that it follows the opening action of the door. It then falls out dramatically to point to the opener in an accusing manner. A particularly nice effect for the liquor cabinet.

46

And while on the subject of arms and the man, don't forget to pick up a fake "broken arm" cast, available in joke shops everywhere. It is the front half of a plaster cast, held on to the arm by elastic straps at the back. When the arm is held across the chest, it is indistinguishable from a real broken-arm cast.

It's best to employ this gimmick with subtlety. Always take one with you on skiing trips; you never know when you may need a little extra sympathy. Wear it around the ski lounge for a couple of nights, then place large bets and challenge some wimp to arm-wrestle.

Maybe you can even work out some help for yourself in the bathroom on the flight back, if you have a gullible flight attendant.

47

The "thread-through-the-jacket back" trick is an unusual gag. You wear a trick shirt that has been cut off halfway up the chest. Over this you button a jacket so everything looks normal. The inside jacket pocket contains a reel of cotton (the same color as the shirt) from which you run a thread over your shoulder and (using a needle) through the jacket in the center of your back.

You then approach your victim and, with a straight

face, point over your shoulder to the thread and ask if he or she could oblige by pulling the thread through. The victim will pull but instead of tugging out an inch or two, yards of cotton will be unreeled. Encourage him to keep pulling and after about six yards the victim will suggest checking your shirt. You open your jacket to reveal the truncated shirt and a bare midriff.

Ordinarily this is not overwhelmingly funny as it makes you the dupe, not the other guy. The hilarity comes in selecting the right victim and occasion. For example, you are the best man at a wedding. Pull this one on the groom immediately on arriving at the church (but before you try the old "tap washer/wedding ring substitution" gambit). A little lighthearted fun dispels nervous tension. Trust me. I know.

The actress Ethel Barrymore once remarked that "you grow up the day you have the first real laugh at yourself." Ethel was way off target on this one, but do try to show the same good-natured grace that you would like to see in your victim.

48

Strolling through the "city of brotherly love" (San Francisco) one day, I was pleased to see an information booth. A deserted information booth. I looked at Harris. Harris looked back at me. We bruised ourselves trying to be the first behind the counter.

I advised a couple from Boise, Idaho, to ask for the local specialty of sourdough hamburger buns. Harris hoped for a San Francisco fog for a pair of newlyweds so that they could enjoy the renowned "harbor cruise by fog light." I recommended that a Texan ride the cable cars of the much-loved Mason–Dixon line. Harris reminded a Japanese tourist to try out the world-famous echo in the Public Library main reading room.

San Francisco is a fine city, but surely it has no right to call that twisty section of Lombard Street between

Hyde and Leavenworth "the crookedest street in the world." That distinction belongs without doubt to New York's Wall Street.

49

Fill a cupboard full of ping-pong balls, so that they flow forth in a tidal wave when the door is opened. The more balls you have, the better. About $25 worth is enough for a good start. You can spread out the cost of the balls across several different victims. Have your camera handy to record the dupe as he opens the cupboard. Fill the cupboard by slipping a thin sheet of cardboard up the front and piling the balls behind it. Shut the door and withdraw the cardboard.

This prank also works well in a locker room. Let your victim hang his clothes in a locker, and while he is absent fill the locker with every kind of ball (large and small) available. It is easier to fill a locker that is laying flat on its back. The victim returns exhausted from his sporty exertions, opens the door to grab his towel, and is carried off in an avalanche of balls.

50

Paint a soap bar thoroughly with several coats of shellac, so that it doesn't get wet and hence won't lather. Leave it out for your friends. Or take it to the locker room and give it to the foambrain you pulled the "ball avalanche" gag on. He's more likely to be taken in if you hand him the soap replaced in its original wrapper.

51

I guess I enjoy throwing everything from a party to a blue fit, and a lot in between. If you are bored, or just looking for new skills, here are three more ideas to throw around. These pastimes are unusual enough to qualify as pranks.

Firstly, try juggling.* If you have enough savvy to tie your own shoelaces, you can learn to juggle in a morning. If you are a member of the clergy, allow up to a week. If you are a senior manager with a Fortune 500 company, do not even attempt any of these stunts.

After the initial learning period you can spend a lifetime mastering advanced juggling tricks. At present I practice differential juggling—that is, juggling dissimilar objects (e.g. a bar of soap, the neighbor's kitten, and a wastepaper basket).

Second, if you are sure you don't have any Freudian hang-ups, try boomeranging. The same people who publish the klutz juggling book also publish a "teach yourself to throw boomerangs" book,† which comes with a simple wooden boomerang. Boomeranging is much harder than juggling. With juggling, you risk back strain picking up dropped objects; with boomeranging, you risk being battered around the head by a whirling lump of wood.

Finally, try a luminous Frisbee (most large toy stores stock this variety, or paint your own). Get a group of people together and throw it around after dark. Recharge the luminosity periodically with a camera flashgun or a flashlight (behind your back, so you don't lose night vision). For some reason this seems to work better indoors, say in a dormitory corridor, and it is especially mirthful if the players have just limbered up by walking back from a bar.

*The best book to teach juggling is *Juggling for the Complete Klutz*, by John Cassidy and B. C. Rimbeaux, published by Klutz Press of Palo Alto, ISBN 0-932592-00-7.

†The best book to teach boomerang throwing is *The Boomerang Book*, also by John Cassidy and published by Klutz Press, ISBN 0-932592-07-4.

52

And speaking of throwing a party, I prepared a unique surprise to greet guests for the last party I held. A friend had a music synthesizer that could be programmed to make amazing sound effects. The synthesizer had a "trigger" feature—an input plug that would start the preprogrammed sound from a remote switch. It was the work of a few minutes to reroute my doorbell wire into the synthesizer input trigger. I then placed the loud-speaker on the garage roof aimed at the front door five feet away. The final part of the trick was selecting the right sound effect. I eventually settled on the "Great Roar of Doom."

Guests pressing the doorbell triggered the sound of a jumbo jet engine, apparently exploding immediately overhead. The soirée really got off to a flying start with most people wanting a stiff brandy as their first drink.

53

There are many more accessories specifically designed for gags: revolving bow ties, handshake "joy buzzers," black soap, plastic barf, blood capsules, whoopee cushions, fake fried eggs, and so on. Most of these are fairly boring in themselves, but can be real winners when used imaginatively.

For example, place a half-full cup of water under a fake stick-on tap, so it is apparently dripping. Sip from the glass occasionally. The fake stick-on tap is particularly effective on the side of objects that genuinely contain liquid, such as an aquarium, rain barrel, or cistern.

I once applied a stick-on tap to the bell of my saxophone, complete with a glass of water underneath; it took a week before my sax instructor even noticed it, then he wanted to photograph the ensemble for the sax-players magazine, *Windbag* or *Sucking Wind* or whatever it's called. But he was blind to humor anyway. At the end of one lesson, I played John Cage's composition "4 minutes 33 seconds"* at 45 rpm instead of 33 rpm, and he didn't notice that either.

*A composer of a decidedly modern school, Cage composed this score to consist entirely of silence for the specified period.

Computer
Capers

The world of computer science seems to attract capable young people, often as talented at pranks as at programming. The term *hacker* was coined to refer to this type of person, and *hacking* to his or her activities.

Hacking used to mean "skillful and creative programming." It was a compliment to be called a hacker. Sadly, the term has now been degraded by media misuse to mean "ignorant poking around with phone access to a remote computer." Hacking in its vintage form deserves a book to itself, but this isn't it. When this chapter talks about hacks, it is referring to the classical meaning.

Only a very simple familiarity with computers is needed to understand most of the pranks in this chapter. To understand absolutely everything you must either be a hacker or be able to count up to twenty without removing your shoes and socks. You should be able to use most of these ideas right away on any system you use and share with other people (it's not much fun playing practical jokes on yourself).

54

There are several hacks relating to computer games, but one of my favorites is the really-good-game-that-takes-forever-to-load. This is a trick program, stored in a directory with other games. The file name should be interesting and suggestive of a really good game (e.g., "BUMZAP," "KILLER," or "SEXTOY"). When the dupe runs this game, the following dialogue occurs:

GAME: "Loading data file . . ."
  (several seconds pass)
GAME: "Still loading . . . continue (Y/N)?"
DUPE: "Y"
  (several more seconds)
GAME: "Overlaying text . . ."
  (several more seconds)
GAME: "Initializing data structures . . . Continue (Y/N)?"
DUPE: "Y"
  (a still longer wait)
GAME: "Almost done . . ."
  (a minute passes)
GAME: "Meltdown . . ."
  etc.

You get the idea. The game never does finish loading, since it is merely a collection of print statements interspersed with delay loops. Really good games are large pieces of software that genuinely take a long time to load, so they maintain player interest by giving this kind of progress report. The joke here is in seeing how long it takes the dupe to realize that this game will *never* finish loading.

You can maintain dupe interest for much longer by programming a more sophisticated dialogue, which hints at the wonders to come. Inquire, for instance, whether the user wants voice control, 3-D animation, and laser hologram graphics. By the time the dupe has replied to scads of questions like these, he has invested so much effort in loading the game that he really wants to see it run. Harden yourself against his inevitable tantrum.

55

I logged onto the DEC-20® computer one day, and the system announced that there was electronic mail for me. I typed in the "MAIL" command to take a look.

There was a short delay while the mail file was retrieved. The short delay lengthened into a minute or so. The bigger the mail file, the longer it takes to retrieve it, so I knew that this must be a truly humongous letter. The previous week one of the jokers from the numerical analysis group had mailed me a letter whose text was a huge and useless Fortran program, to waste my time in exactly this way. I suspected that this was a repeat performance of the same gag. Eventually the mailer finished reading the file and started displaying it to me.

The text of the letter seemed to consist of nothing but "forwarding notices." In electronic mail systems there is a command that forwards a newly received letter to an additional addressee. The mail system adds a couple of lines at the beginning, explaining who asked for this letter to be forwarded.

This letter was thousands of lines long. Almost all of these lines were forwarding notices. It had been forwarded between hundreds of different users on scores of different host machines. It had been sent over computer networks all across the country. Each person who forwarded the letter caused it to grow larger by a couple of lines.

I finally reached the end of all the thousands of lines of forwarding notices, and read the text. It was a brief notice to the effect that the recipient should "forward this letter to two people you know on any computer system to which you can network. It is bad luck if you break the chain." This was an electronic chain letter!

Electronic mail offers most of the features of ordinary mail, and so it was not too surprising that junk mail eventually appeared. This chain letter had been running for several months and had spread to so many different hosts that, like a virus, it had a life of its own and is probably still circulating today. Of course, if any system manager wanted to punish this misuse of machine resources, he need only look at a copy of the letter to see an exact trail of who sent it. . . .

56

Most computer systems have a special start-up file that is automatically executed when the user reboots the system or logs on. Under the Unix® operating system the file is called ".login"; for DEC VAX/VMS® it is "login.com"; on the IBM/PC® it is "autoexec.bat"; the IBM MVS/TSO® operating system uses "LIB.CLIST(@LOGON)"; it is "PROFILE.EXEC" for VM/CMS®, and so on.

A practical joker can place extra commands into the start-up file, which will be executed along with the genuine commands. For a real zinger, make the last of your extra commands restore the start-up file to its state before you hacked it (by copying the saved original version to overwrite your hacked version). Your victim will thus find no trace of how the hack was done. You need write permission to change someone's start-up file. The easiest way to achieve this is to wait until the victim goes away from his terminal for a few minutes, then slip over and grant yourself this privilege by using his account.

One morning I logged onto my Unix account and was startled to see a picture of a rocket being launched on my terminal. This was a really first-class hack, imaginative and original. The perpetrator had prepared a text file that was a simple line drawing of a rocket standing vertically. It was about a hundred lines long, roughly four screens full. Then he inserted a command into every start-up file on the system, to type out this file. The next time each user logged on, the file containing the drawing of the rocket was typed on his screen. As the terminal scrolled upward, it created the illusion that the rocket was rising off the top of the screen. Sheer poetry. Given this basic idea, it is possible to craft ruder programs, such as a rising finger or other bodily appendages.

There are many other hacks possible through using start-up files or other Trojan horses. For instance, you could make the file type out a rude greeting to the user ("What do you want, snotnose?") or change the system prompt (one creative and hopeful undergraduate crafted a multiline prompt that was a representation of an erect male member together with the demand "eat me!"). An anonymous hacker at Yale specialized in editing start-up files so that they shut off the system. This is done by making the first line of the start-up file be a "log off" command. As soon as the user logs on, the system executes the start-up file that immediately logs him off (or spins down the disk on a PC).

How do you ever recover from this? Most systems have a "quick log on" option that lets you log on without executing the start-up file. There also is a slim chance that the system interrupt key can break in after you have logged on, but before the start-up file has been executed. Failing this, someone else must remove or overwrite the errant command file for you. Don't be cruel, this hack is too brutal to unleash on anyone except an expert user.

Finally you could fix the login file so that the terminal gives the impression that it is deleting all of the users files. Have it ignore attempts to stop it. This makes even an experienced user become rather agitated. Take the most stringent care that you only *simulate* deletion (through printing out a text file that looks the same as the delete command results). Never actually delete anybody's files, as that crosses the boundary from prank into serious vandalism.

To protect yourself against becoming the victim of one of these hacks, never leave your terminal logged on and unattended; ensure that you are the only user who has write access to your start-up file. No foolproof protection is possible on an unsophisticated computer such as the IBM/PC, although newer systems like the IBM PS/2 support passwords.

57

There is a wide range of computer tricks that can only be pulled on inexperienced users. I saw one of the best in my first day as a graduate student in the Yale computer-science department. A senior graduate student had set up (and "set up" is the right phrase) an introduction to the department facilities. He described the artificial-intelligence laboratory and invited someone to try their latest and greatest program: a system that could converse like a human being, over a terminal. We were expecting great things, and someone volunteered to converse with it. Unbeknownst to us (but knownst to the demonstrator) the "program" was actually an accomplice in the back of the room typing responses over a terminal. The conversation started like this:

GRADUATE STUDENT: "Hello"

FAKE AI PROGRAM: "Hi! What would you like to discuss?"

GRADUATE STUDENT: "Wow! Is the stock market going up or down?"

FAKE AI PROGRAM: (apparently thinks for a few seconds)
"Yes! But not right away . . ."

We were greatly impressed, and continued to think up new questions for this oracle to answer.

The demonstration ended abruptly with the following exchange:

GRADUATE STUDENT: "What is a proton?"

FAKE AI PROGRAM: (shooting right back)
"It's a professional weight. Haha, only kidding! Did you know you have a zit on your nose, and your mother dresses you funny."

Since that day, I have always had a healthy skepticism about claims made for artificial-intelligence software.

58

Many computer games maintain a "high score" list. The top half-dozen players have their names and scores displayed to each person who starts the game. It provides some minor glory and a target for the other players to beat.

It's always a good idea to fix the high-score list so that if your victim gets on it, an unflattering message also appears. Something like "wasting more time, eh Dave?" or "after only 267 attempts, finally on the high-score list." Or fix it so his real score is replaced by a truly worthless score.

The fix can be to reprogram the code that writes the high-score list (hard if you don't have the source code of the game), or to amend the high-score list after the game is finished (easier).

59

All multi-user computer systems have a facility that allows one user to send a message to another user's terminal. Usually the message is preceded by the sender's log-in ID, but a new user will often not recognize the ID of one of his colleagues. Working as a contract programmer on a large Unisys mainframe, I was suddenly confronted by a message on my terminal saying: "Operations Department: Computability quota exceeded—log off now."

It was so official looking. But what on earth is a "computability quota" and how much of it do I have before it is used up? In desperation, I sought my project leader. "Are they serious about this?" I asked anxiously. "No," he replied after seeing the sender ID, "but he is," motioning to a colleague choking with suppressed laughter at an adjacent terminal.

60

The greatest all-time computer practical joke I have seen to date was the Crumble program. Created by a talented and imaginative Yale student, Crumble ran on a bit-mapped graphics system. Bit-mapped graphics are a high-resolution form of output, which allow great control over the image displayed.

When the Crumble program was run, it manipulated the graphics memory. Its effect was to slowly pulverize the image on the terminal screen. It looked exactly as though minute fragments of the letters were gradually breaking off and drifting to the bottom of the screen, where they accumulated as piles of "dust." After a few minutes, the screen would be totally blank except for piles of dust on the bottom line. This is very disconcerting. These lines on the screen have no physical reality; they are merely phosphor particles that glow when excited by a cathode ray. Yet here they are apparently falling off the screen like dried ashes.

The prank worked like this: you waited until one of your colleagues left his terminal unattended, then you went up and started the Crumble program. Crumble ran as a background job, leaving the terminal free to accept further commands. The colleague would return to continue with his work, and gradually notice the display was turning to powder. The effect was so subtle, unexpected, and well implemented that people thought it was a hardware fault and could not believe they had been hacked.

Crumble inspired several variants, of which the best known was Worms. Instead of crumbling the screen, Worms gave the impression that it was being tunneled through and eaten by worms. Hackers could set parameters controlling the number of worms and their size and speed. Worms, in turn, led to a zinger. We had four terminals side by side on a table in the terminal room. One hacker carefully amended the Worms program and positioned the screens so that the four terminals were treated in a coordinated way. He started Worms, and observers were startled to see a single large worm undulate across the first terminal and into the second (and subsequent screens) at the same rhythm and pace. It looked exactly like a long snake squirming from one side of the room to the other, only visible where it passed through the terminals.

The Crumble and Worm programs were two really splendid hacks. They have not become widespread because they require significant programming effort, and they are only possible on bit-mapped graphics systems (which are still relatively uncommon). Crumble and Worm were implemented on the Yale GEM system several years before the IBM/PC was developed. Inferior versions of the two programs are now available for the IBM/PC.

A related hack is a short program I have seen that changes the cursor on an IBM/PC to be a moving bar. It is most unnerving to see a normally motionless cursor gliding silently up and down. When the victim comments on it, it is etiquette to suggest that he check whether the vertical hold on the cathode ray beam might be breaking down.

61

When all your most sophisticated programming pranks are thwarted, it sometimes pays to get back to basics. Prize off and exchange two keys on your victim's terminal keyboard. Most programmers are not touch-typists, and they look at the keyboard to find keys. For best

---

*Oh no! The stupid footnotes have come back again.

effect swap two keys that are not commonly used (not letters or numbers—it's too easy to notice they are misplaced), e.g., the colon/semicolon or tilde/accent keys. Alternatively, if possible, put one key on upside down.

This was once done to me in a multihardware environment, where one dumb terminal was connected through various networks to many different pieces of hardware. People would often see bizarre characters echoed if the different protocols, speeds, baud rates, etc. didn't match. Expecting the fault to be in the network, I never suspected my terminal. I spent ages fruitlessly checking all these parameters before I finally realized what had happened.

It was Tom the wicked system manager (with the stained tie) who played this trick on me, and he followed it up with a zinger a few weeks later. He amended my start-up file, changing my system prompt (usually set to "you are a tiger") to write the last word in high-intensity double-height flashing characters. He stopped by my terminal the next day to crow and was dumbfounded to learn that his hack hadn't worked. He investigated twenty different possible reasons (maybe I had discovered the hack in advance, perhaps I had adjusted the terminal characteristics, possibly the transmission line was dropping extra escape characters). I let him stew on it for a week, and then I broke the news that the graphics capability on this terminal had burnt out a few weeks previously and I hadn't bothered replacing it. I had boomeranged his zinger.

62

A favorite fantasy of every computer programmer is to write a games program and implement a secret keystroke that will make the player invincible. The programmer can then challenge all comers, but (using his secret command) will never be beaten at his own game. This fantasy is rarely achieved because it is such a big job to write or amend a large computer program.

One Christmas, I achieved the secret keystroke game fantasy. I took a table-tennis ("Pong") game that came with a PC as a demonstration program and hacked it so that typing the magic word "XYZZY" would cause the computer to play itself. That is, the computer would bounce the ball off the back wall in an attempt to dodge the bat, but the computer would also guide the bat in an attempt to hit the ball.

Initially, I wrote the program so that when the ball bounced off the far wall, the computer would calculate the angle of reflection, use trigonometry to predict where it would strike, and move the bat directly there. When I switched to the secret undefeatable mode, the superior performance was too obvious: people simply cannot predict a bounce that well. So I changed the algorithm. I made the bat move so that its horizontal component was always the same as that of the ball. The bat tracked the ball across the screen and no matter how fast the ball traveled, the bat was always in the right place to return the serve. If the player continued to press the keys, he would be ignored but it would look as though he was still controlling the game.

I could hardly wait till my friend Harris next came over to my house. I served a couple of beers and suggested trying the newly acquired Pong game. After a few practice sessions, we started to compete in earnest. Harris managed a respectable score and stood back for my turn. I started playing, then typed the secret command to flip the game into invincible mode. Harris's eyes grew wider and rounder as my score rolled up higher and higher. At last I took pity on him. In the midst of a fast and desperate play, I took both hands off the keyboard, turned completely away from the screen, and picked up my beer to drink it. The bat continued moving as fast as ever, and my score continued to mount. Harris's face turned the exact shade of the number-five truck at the Long Hill fire station, and he swore he'd never trust computers again. He already knew better than to put his faith in me.

63

Most computer games are tedious time-wasters, but occasionally some aspect is interesting enough to hold a hacker's attention. For instance, backgammon is the only game in which a computer has beaten the reigning human world champion. About ten years ago chess programs were only as good as a county-level player; now the best chess programs play at the level of an international master. It is quite possible that chess programs will beat grand masters within a few years. Part of the problem for human players is that computers play with an unexpected style that some players find difficult to penetrate. It's called "exhaustive analysis of all the moves likely to lead to a win."

Every year the Association for Computer Machinery holds a computer chess championship* and the top programs slug it out. This is the major league, with programs such as HITECH using a Sun work station with special-purpose hardware, and BLITZ running on the CRAY X/MP, the world's most powerful computer. I find it fascinating to think of these supercomputer titans computing furiously against one another over a checkered board.

Many programs have been written to play card games, including blackjack, bridge, cribbage, and of course poker. A fellow hacker once told me that he suspected a particular poker-playing program was cheating. I told him that this was entirely consistent with the history and tradition of the game. You can't play good poker unless you know how to deal from the bottom of the deck.

How could software cheat? It could look at the "cards" it had dealt you and then select good cards for itself from the remainder of the deck. Actually it wouldn't even have to do this. It could just remember all the

---

*Refer to "Communications of the ACM," 30:7, July 1987, pages 640 to 645 for an exciting description of a computer chess championship.

cards it had legitimately seen, and hence deduce what cards remained to be played. It could then estimate the probability of getting the cards it needed for a winning hand, and play accordingly. This is exactly what expert card players do anyway, but the computer has a perfect memory and can do it faster, and more accurately.

It is an intriguing idea to write a program that deliberately cheats. Cardsharping is too easy. I would suggest a chess program that, say once per game, repositions one of its pieces or secretly removes an opposing piece as well as taking its normal turn. See how long it takes before the human opponent catches it.

64

A large part of my career has been spent as a software engineer programming various compilers. Compiler writing is fun. On a scale of one to ten, it comes in a little way behind a cool beer on a hot day. Well, actually quite a long way behind. It's difficult, challenging work, and every other programmer on the system gets to use your handiwork. If it doesn't always provide enough of a stimulus by itself, you can always program in extra hacks.

I remember doing development work on a Pascal compiler in November. It was the day before my birthday. As an afterthought before going home, I wrote a truly unique hack to greet me the following morning. I coded a few dozen lines of code that would cause the compiler to play (using the terminal bell) the tune of "Happy Birthday" on the first compilation every November 14. The tune was a bit monotonic—you could do better on a PC—but it was certainly a unique compiler feature.

How much more user-friendly can you get? This particular modification never made it into the production version of the compiler, but it did impress my coworkers.

As I was writing this book, I took a draft of this chapter in to work to show to some colleagues, and I put it on the computer system. The next day, the contents of the file had been removed and replaced with the following message:

Jokes That Have Backfired

One day, a fine day in summer, the author's boss read a funny story he was working on when he was supposed to be programming, and the boss decided to fire the author. The big boss guy thought this was very very funny, as did all the other guys in the research lab.

The boss guy was a bit concerned that this might delay production of all the other chapters, but he need not have worried because the author now had so much free time that he had problems keeping the book to a reasonable length.

Write on Peter!!!

What a boomerang! I made discreet inquiries and discovered the architect of this prank was not my boss, but a co-worker. It was the revenge for a login file hack I had played on him months before. I had written a small program to play "space music" and draw flying saucers all over his terminal. Jeez! Some people just can't take a joke.

College
Collage

As everyone knows, universities are tremendous storehouses of knowledge: each year the freshmen bring in a tiny amount of learning, and the departing seniors take none away.

A university is the place where many young people first find out what independence really means; that is, being totally broke, and at the same time having to take care of their own dirty laundry. They are still defining the limits of their capabilities and tolerance for sitting up all night discussing obscure foreigners, such as the sultry Spanish girl in the Math 101 class, with the long dark curly teeth.

Undergraduates have an abundance of time, energy, and opportunity, but they can't spend all their time in bed with their friends. So it's not surprising that some of the most ingenious practical jokes have been created in a college environment.

66

In Cambridge, England, there is a bridge over the river Cam with a parapet on which rested four large stone balls, about the size of beach balls. One of these balls has been missing for years. A group of undergraduates secretly replaced the weighty ornament with a painted polystyrene equivalent. It looked identical, but weighed about as much as a handful of feathers.

These miscreants then waited until a boat came down the river, heading directly under the fake stone orb. The students rushed up to the parapet and made a great show of trying to dislodge the ball onto the boat below. One student even whipped out a crowbar and strained against the "stone." The panic-stricken passengers in the boat jumped into the river, which is about two feet deep at this point, while the crowd above gave a final push and cheered as the polystyrene "stone" ball floated gently downward.

67

In Cambridge, Massachusetts, stands the Massachusetts Institute of Technology, probably the foremost scientific university in the world. The students are among the smartest and most talented young scientists in the U.S.A., and they play pranks to match. One of the M.I.T buildings is the Meteorology Tower, a twenty-story building topped off with a huge spherical radar dome.

One year, a small group of undergraduates decided that the Cambridge skyline needed brightening up. They carefully made their preparations, and a few mornings later Cambridge woke up to find a huge yellow "smiley face" staring down from the radar dome. The students had painted the face onto a massive yellow tarpaulin, secretly taken this to the top of the tower, picked the lock to the roof, and secured it over the dome. Actually, it's not so all-fired hard to pick a lock. Simply use the index finger of your right hand to point directly at the lock and say in a loud voice, "*That's* the one I want."

68

Students are not the only pranksters within a university. When my brother Paul was taking undergraduate geology, also known as "Rocks for Jocks," I gave him detailed and careful advice on how to handle his *viva voce* (oral examination). I explained that when the professor hands you an exhibit, even if you know what it is at once, you don't just blurt out the answer. You should turn the object over in your hands thoughtfully for a minute or so, frown slightly as if deep in thought, and then say, "Well, I've never seen anything *exactly* like this, but it has certain characteristics that remind me of . . . ," and so on.

Paul duly went into the examination room, was given a rock, and started his big performance. He must have hammed it up too much, because after half a minute, the professor snapped pettishly, "For goodness sake, get on with it; it's only a lump of coal."

The next time he took an oral examination, they obviously thought they should give him an exhibit worthy of such a bravura performance. He got a meteorite; the rock wasn't even from planet Earth.

69

The Sterling Memorial Library of Yale University (so named to commemorate the once great currency of the British Pound Sterling. Ha-ha! Just kidding; it is actually named after the great Yale benefactor, Bob Memorial-Library) is an imposing building topped by a tower with a row of thirteen tall narrow windows. The windows are like parallel slits in the tower, several stories high.

An ingenious group of Ezra Stiles College undergraduates noticed the window configuration and had the idea of lighting selected panes in these tall windows to produce letters and words. Computer dot-matrix printers work on the same principle; from a distance the neighboring dots (or points of light, in the case of the windows) merge to form letters. The phrase would have to be short, because of the limited width of the windows.

One night, the students hid in the book stacks until the library closed. They then ran all over the tower placing lanterns in windowpanes according to a prearranged plan. When they had finished, there blazed forth from the tower a strident message, at once brief, original, and challenging; "FORK OFF" it would have read, if the middle two letters were something other than you see.

I thought this was just another apocryphal story. But a couple of years after hearing it, I saw a poster showing the Sterling Library at twilight, and in the center, unobtrusive but present if you looked for it, this message of defiance was shining forth over the cross-campus quadrangle.

70

The doors to individual bedrooms in college dorms are usually fitted with spy holes to let the occupant see who is outside, for security reasons. A much-loved lark is to pin up a poster over the outside of your door, making a small hole in it where the door viewer pokes through. Align one eye on the pinup's face with the door viewer.

People passing in the corridor are thus treated to the sight of some film star or other poster creature, staring out through a monocle on your door. If you are totally lacking inhibitions and good taste (fortunately there are still a few of us left like this), then you need not restrict yourself to positioning the viewer through a eye on the poster. You can use more varied parts of the anatomy. If challenged, claim that you are a modern artist, and this is a social comment on dorm life.

71

A fine prank, which can still be seen, is the "Harvard Bridge measurement." The Harvard Bridge is a very long bridge over the Charles River basin near M.I.T.

A few years ago, the freshmen pledging to an M.I.T. fraternity were given the task of measuring the length of the Harvard Bridge in units of "Smoots." Smoot was the shortest person in the entering freshman class.

Accordingly, the pledgees picked up young Smoot and laid him end to end across the entire length of the bridge. Every fifty Smoots they painted a line on the sidewalk. After all, you wouldn't want to have to start from the beginning again if you lost count halfway or if your measuring stick burst free and ran off. The bridge measures 364.4 Smoots, plus an ear. Every year the Smoot markers are repainted by the new pledging froshers.

72

At college, I first learned to ride a unicycle. On a scale of 1 to 10, this feat is about a 26½. Dormitory corridors are ideal for beginning unicycle jockeys. They are long and straight, and fairly empty during the day. You tend to fall over rather a lot when starting out, so you appreciate the solitude. I eventually became skilled enough to found the "YALEJURDS" club; the Yale-All England, Juggling, Unicycle Racing, and Dangerous Sports club. But, as the builder said when he saw the plans for an extra penthouse, that's another story.

My master coup was in persuading my extremely rotund friend Den to try the unicycle. Den really was a blimp, a bowling ball with feet, but he was always game to try new things. He didn't so much straddle the monowheel as absorb it upwards into his midriff. I took the precaution of relabeling the door to the girls' bathroom as "storeroom." "Aim to stop against that locked storeroom door, Den" was my final advice.

Having such a low center of gravity seemed to give him a small natural advantage. But only at low speed. He pushed off and wobbled uneasily down the passage, like a sumo wrestler with a drinking problem. He picked up speed as he went and started to oscillate a bit. He would have made it safely, I really think he would, if only he hadn't foolishly tried to stop by running into the bathroom door.

Den hit the door like a freight train slamming into a henhouse. The door flew open under his pudgy impact. Den pitched forward, the unicycle shot backward, and under the momentum Den slid across the wet floor straight into a shower stall. Which was a considerable surprise for the music student taking a shower within. Weeks after, she explained that she had been to a "Save the Whales" rally the day before, and her first thought was that a whale had now come for her. As I told Den later that day, when everything was finally straightened out and the university police had left, I didn't think there were notes above high C.

After that, I used to practice alone in the early hours of the night. Cornering is the most difficult aspect of unicycle riding; you have to keep the speed up, but that introduces balancing problems. I reasoned that if only I could spin the wheel fast enough, I'd be the torque of the town. If people came to their doors to see what all the noise was, I told them that I was thinking of buying a bicycle but wanted to master one wheel first before working my way up to two. Similarly those learning to ski are advised to just try one ski at first.

73

On my first day at Manchester University in England, I went to the student union building to look around. Entering the bar, I had to step over the supine form of a large bearded upperclassman stretched out drunk on the floor. In the gloom, at first I thought it was one of those bearskin rugs, complete with an ugly snarling ferocious animal head. When I realized that it was a fellow student, my soul was filled with hope; could the beer here really be cheap enough and strong enough to do this?

There's no substitute for experience, so I got to work at once. Which reminded me of the feeble practical joke I had seen earlier in the day. A large hand-printed notice had been affixed to the wall in the middle of a long corridor. FRESHMEN: WAIT HERE it instructed. It was fooling no one. A for conception, F for execution.

74

Here are a few ideas for those backward outposts of antique tutelage still using blackboards and chalk.

Wedge small fragments of chalk into the board eraser. When the pedagogue wipes the board, he will actually put more chalk on instead of clearing it. Nuns in particular hate this. But be careful; nuns always exact terrible vengeance.

This trick is for those blackboards that are a continuous loop, like a conveyer belt running up one wall. Place pieces of chalk all along the ledges separating the board panels. When the teacher pulls down on the board to bring a fresh section into view, voilà, chalk and chalk dust shower onto his head.

Finally, there is the old chestnut of writing slogans or pictures on the reverse side of a blackboard. When teacher needs another board and swivels it over, he is confronted with the kindergarten equivalent of wit. Dumbfound your classics teacher with poetry such as:

> Latin is a language
> As dead as dead can be.
> It killed the ancient Romans,
> And now it's killing me!

or the always boring:

> Those who can, do
> Those who can't, teach!
> Those who can't teach, teach teachers!
> Those who can't teach teachers, teach gym!

Don't be too offensive; teachers have a pretty rough job during the hours they are actually working. I would rather retire to the Bahamas on $1 million a year than spend a day teaching ninth grade.

75

At Manchester University I was allocated to a freshman dormitory with Bob. All freshman like to live a little wild at first, but Bob seemed to be making a career out of it. He had been kicked out of Cambridge University at the end of his first year, and now he was repeating his freshman year at Manchester. He was also repeating all the antics that got him kicked out of Cambridge.

To describe Bob as a filthy debauched rascal is like saying that St. Francis was generally a good man. Yes, and then some. Bob used to time his cooking by waiting for the kitchen smoke alarm to go off. When Bob made tea, he put all the ingredients, water, tea bags, milk, sugar, into the kettle and boiled the whole thing up together. He said it saved time. Bob once decided to experiment with how long he could go without washing or having a haircut. The burden of this project chiefly and unfairly fell on his roommates.

One night, Bob returned late from a night of drinking. Harris and I decided to intervene, and we gave Bob a hair trim as he lay dead drunk in bed. Bob never said anything about it the next day, but a week later he returned from similar revelries with one of his friends from another university. He complained bitterly that on waking the morning after, he had noticed that someone had cut his hair.

His grooming was evidently so infrequent that it had taken a week for him to notice. Harris told him not to be such a damn fool. Bob would have been a prime candidate for the shellac-coated soap (ruse number 50). We could also have tied his two big toes to the foot of the bed with twine. This gives a drunkard considerable exercise when he tries to get up in the morning.

76

One practical joke that works well in lectures, talks, or presentations is to flash up a slide at the start giving some ridiculously fancy title, such as:

"Comparative Trends in Greek Philosophy and Pizza"
or
"String: Uses and Abuses in Western Culture"
or
"Adaptive Photosynthesis in the Amazin'
Rainforests of Salford"

or even

"Twisted Polynomial HyperAlgebras: facts
for the under-5's"

Apologize briefly and explain that this is "another one of my little interests," implying that the real subject of your talk is also merely another one of your little interests. . . .

Even if you are not the person giving the talk, you can infiltrate the slide anyway.

77

The time had arrived for the 1980 Yale computer-science graduate students to give talks on their independent research projects. We got together beforehand and discussed our various approaches. After we had settled all this serious business, our meeting relaxed a bit. Lenny suggested that we confound the faculty (the scourge of graduate students everywhere) by having every one of us include the word *rutabaga* at some point in each talk.

The first time it occurred, nobody would notice anything, but by the third or fourth time the faculty would puzzle over what was happening, and eventually they would be listening for the word. Our plan would add levity to an otherwise dry and serious afternoon of presentations.

At first everything went according to plan. As each successive student mentioned the word *rutabaga*, a buzz of increasing consternation swept through the assembled body of professors. The last student stood up and began his talk. It was Lenny, the originator of the rutabaga idea. Everyone leaned forward expectantly, but Lenny plowed on to the end of his presentation without once mentioning the vegetable.

The session broke up with cheers and laughter over this stunning omission. As we left the lecture hall, a professor in the corridor asked what all the excitement was about. "Lenny never said *rutabaga* in his research talk" was the singular reply.

Theatrical
Tricks

Ah, the theater. They say that once you experience life behind the green door, you're hooked forever. The attractions are legion. The bright lights, the dancing girls, the roar of the greasepaint, the smell of the crowd, and the most enchanting sound of all, the beloved sound heard by each actor at the end of every performance: the rustle of the takings being counted in the box office.

There is a long and honorable tradition of trickery and hoaxes within the theater. Virtually every Shakespearean play relies on one or more ruses to advance the plot. These ruses are always carefully spelled out to the audience in advance, since the Elizabethan theater in its day was roughly the cultural equivalent of, say, television game shows. I have long felt that some of these tricks were rather overplayed.

Take, for example, that courtroom scene in *The Merchant of Venice* where Portia is denying Shylock his pound of flesh by arguing that if he also draws blood with it, he'll be in the slammer before you could say "St. Mark's Square (but the other apostles are very trendy)." If I had been representing Shylock on that day, there would have been a very different outcome. Liposuction cosmetic surgery would have pulled that pound of flesh quicker than a New York minute. At the very least Shylock should have taken the case to the court of appeal.

Theater folk are by nature gregarious and extroverted. They take to pranks as though to the manner born. But you must be sporting. Only play around with pranks and tricks in rehearsals. Or at the absolute limit, during a dress rehearsal. Never, never do it during a live performance. Unless your victim is truly asking for it.

78

Here's a jest that's more fun than the second law of thermodynamics.* You need to be on stage with your victim, and you need to be carrying a glass or drinking tumbler. Upstage your victim in the play by showily placing the glass right on the edge of a table just before you exit.

The audience's attention will be wholly taken up with staring at the glass to see if it will fall. Maybe that's why they're called "tumblers." Anybody unlucky enough to be left on stage might just as well be speaking pages from the telephone directory as saying their lines.

What the audience don't know is that you put double-sided sticky type on the base of the glass. It will remain three-quarters off the table from now till God's own drumroll brings down the final curtain.

79

I once took the job of stage manager during a university run of *How the Other Half Loves* by Alan Ayckbourn. This play has a dinner-party scene where an actor samples some avocado purée and has to complain querulously, "It tastes like—canned pineapple."

As stage manager, it was my job to supply the avo-

---

*The second law of thermodynamics was passed by Congress on June 5, 1873. It provides that, "It is impossible by means of inanimate material agency to derive mechanical effort from any portion of matter by cooling it below the temperature of the coldest of the surrounding objects." In layperson's terms: "the universe is gradually winding down, and we don't have a key to wind it up again." Bummer.

cado purée, which I did every night except the last. On the closing night, when the actors were thoroughly accustomed to finding avocado purée on their plates, I substituted, yes, canned pineapple, puréed and dyed green.

They say that the actor gave the most realistic performance of his life, with a real note of puzzled bewilderment in his lines.

I got severely reprimanded by the director afterward, since this type of surprise can throw an actor totally. The director was still cross with me from a few days previously. We had decided that we needed to change the name of one of the characters, to be more indigenous to the U.S. Quick as a flash I suggested the name of my thesis adviser, a professor at the university.

When the show was running, I secured some front-row seats for this man and had the pleasure of watching him freak out when his name cropped up in the play. Of course, having him freak out in the front row for no apparent reason also caused half the cast (the nervy half) to freak out in sympathy.

80

The hit comedy *Noises Off* is always good for unexpected hilarity. The play is about the staging of a play, and concerns the backstage and onstage dramas that occur. The first time you see *Noises Off*, it can be a little disconcerting.

The curtain rises, and a couple on stage conduct a conversation appropriate to their dress and surroundings. Five minutes into this, a man suddenly stands up in the stalls and yells at them. There is total confusion as the audience tries to figure out what to do about this lunatic disrupting the play.

Then one of the actors on stage responds to the ranting lunatic. They carry on a dialogue. The author Michael Frayn has pulled a massive practical joke on the audience. The "lunatic" is acting the part of the director of the play within the play, running a rehearsal from the auditorium. Fantastic!

I first saw *Noises Off* performed in Germany, where they take their theater very seriously indeed. The German title was *Die Nackte Wahnsinn*, which roughly translates as *Naked Illusions*, so I had gone to see the play under a totally mistaken set of assumptions anyway. When the actor playing the director stood up and started shouting at the cast on stage, another member of the audience actually tried to restrain the "lunatic," who he assumed was interfering with the performance. A classic boomerang to a fine practical joke.

81

Woody Allen uses the same dramatic trick, introducing no less than six new characters from the body of the audience, in his play *God*. These characters include a girl, two men and a woman from the audience, and an usherette. The men and the woman debate whether or not they are fictional characters. One of the men ends up storming out of the theater in a huff, demanding his money back. It's all in the script, but it really challenges the audience's credulity. Woody is playing with fire, in planting this idea in the consciousness of a New York audience. Woody also writes a doctor into the script, just to sit in the auditorium and respond affirmatively to the time-honored plea "Is there a doctor in the house?"

God is very much a play to experience rather than just watch; but remember to keep your mouth shut. Having set the scene with several "members of the audience" who are really actors, Woody gives one of the actors some dialogue to go into the audience and ad-lib with two or three real members of the audience, to convince everyone else that they, too, are stooges.

What more could happen? Well, Woody writes himself into the script; and the stage prompter; he brings on Groucho Marx, and the character Blanche Du Bois from Tennessee Williams's play A *Streetcar Named Desire*,* and more besides. If you ever get the chance to see a production of *God*, it's well worth going to.

82

In the fall of 1981, I was flying scenery (pulling backdrop ropes) backstage in a Yale University Theater production of the musical *Chicago*. The play features several shop dummies that appear in one scene and are then put aside. This production ended by raising a curtain to present the backstage orchestra, who play a number to finish the show.

All went well until this closing number of the last night. As the curtain was raised to reveal the orchestra, the seven dummies were raised with it. Someone had inconspicuously tied the feet of the dummies to the bottom rail of the curtain.

The mannequins swung wildly to and fro over the heads of the orchestra members, who played on obliviously. The audience seemed to think it was part of the plot and applauded with great gusto. The effect was everything I hoped for, and I didn't even get a reprimand from the director. She said she liked it so much she would incorporate it into any future performances.

*The streetcar lines in New Orleans were named after the main avenue of the route. Thus there were streetcars named "Desire," "Cemeteries," "Tulane," and so on. For more than twenty years, the sole remaining streetcar line has been the St. Charles Avenue line, but somehow A *Streetcar Named St. Charles* just doesn't have the same ring to it.

83

If you find yourself acting in a play with a prop telephone, don't miss this gag. Arrange for the stage phone to ring unexpectedly. When the cast is thoroughly confused, but before anyone has dropped out of character, answer the phone.

As a zinger, just say "It's for you," and hand it to another member of the cast. The other actors will collapse into uncontrollable laughter, and the director will probably not find it as funny as you do.

Food for
Thought

Some people eat to live; we call these *gourmets*. Others live to eat; we call these *gourmands*. Me, I get lively when I eat and drink; we call this *rowdiness*. These pranks are the fast food of the humor world. And why do they call it "fast food"? Because after you've eaten it, you wish that you'd fasted instead.

I once found the following parable inside a fortune cookie in California.

A disciple asked: "What is Fate, Master?"

And the Master replied: "It is that which gives a reason for the beasts of burden. It is that under which a man must ever toil. It is that which has caused nations to build byways from city to city, upon which carts and coaches pass, and alongside which inns have come to be built to stave off Hunger, Thirst, and Weariness."

"And that is Fate?" said the disciple.

"Fate . . . I thought you said Freight," responded the Master.

"That's all right," said the disciple, "I wanted to know what Freight was, too."

The parable seems to sum up the essence of practical joking in a way that unscrews the unscrutable. The practical jokes here cover ideas from all the five basic food groups, namely liquor, caffeine, salt, grease, and sugar.

84

My good friend J. Y. Kelly comes from Australia, where a major cultural activity is trying to stick your friends with the check at bars and restaurants. Last time we had a Chinese meal together, I cracked open my fortune cookie to find a small note reading: "Confucius says that you would be well advised to pick up the tab for this meal."

This is an easy trick to pull off, because you can buy a box of fortune cookies and prepare your own cracker-barrel homilies in advance. If you want to make the mottoes really authentic, then use a typewriter and reduce them to the right size on a reducing photocopier.

Perennial presidential hopeful Al Haig played this trick at a Washington press conference in September 1987. He handed out fortune cookies to the journalists, who opened them to find inspiring mottoes such as "Al Haig for President" and "Don't be vague, vote for Haig." One motto, in a double bluff of palate-puckering proportions, even claimed "Cookie is delectable, Haig is electable."

Make a meal end with a swing by secretly substituting "adult" fortune cookies ("You will shortly meet an anatomically gifted person of the opposite sex who will attempt to . . ." etc.). You could also prepare insulting fortunes ("Fu Manchu suggests you lose ten pounds of useless ugly fat—cut your head off").

Finally, if you are unable to prepare your own fortune cookies, simply add the phrase *in bed* or *the bed* at the end of reading out whatever motto you really got. For example, "Your troubles will soon be all over" is read out as "Your troubles will soon be all over the bed." "You will develop a successful new business" becomes "You will develop a successful new business in bed." I've only seen one fortune that wasn't improved by this addition. It predicted simply "You will sleep soundly tonight."

85

Create a tub of vegetable yogurt. Cut through the bottom of a regular vanilla yogurt carton with a very sharp knife, and insert some fresh diced vegetables. You need the type of yogurt carton made from waxed paper, with a rim at the bottom. Reseal the package with candle wax.

When the dupe takes it from the fridge and discovers the potatoes, onion, carrots, and yes, rutabaga, explain that you heard something on the radio about a new health-food yogurt being test-marketed in the area.

86

Prepare some sugared almonds for your friends and guests. The joke works especially well on refined but greedy relatives. Take some almonds and prepare a sugar sauce to coat them. Make up several batches of the sugar coating with different food colorings. But . . . in the yellow and blue coatings use pieces of garlic cloves instead of almonds.

Garlic is a potent and tasty flavoring; it's just a little—uh—unexpected in this context. The different colorings allow you to join in the tasty snack without being boomeranged. Don't do this to an elderly aunt of whom you have "great expectations."

87

Here is a practical joke to play on the greediest person you know. Bet him that he cannot eat twelve donuts. It doesn't seem like a lot to a greedy person. The wager should stipulate that if he eats the whole dozen delicious donuts, then you pay for them; if he fails to eat them, then he must buy them, and carry out some trifling forfeit such as paying your mortgage for the next twelve months.

My experience has been that many gluttons are attracted by this bet. The secret to winning is to ensure that your piggish pal drinks plenty of liquid while consuming the donuts. Wait until he has eaten about six, then supply a refreshing beverage. Once he drinks anything at all, he has effectively lost the bet, for the liquid will swell up the dough inside him and prevent further consumption.

The first time I played this trick, I was unaware of the need to get the participant to drink, and it turned into a boomerang for me. The beneficiary of the donut largess was my greedy pal Den. Some people are afraid of heights; after they meet Den, they're afraid of widths, too.

To my astonishment, Den wolfed down the first ten donuts in one straight run. The eleventh was a bit of a struggle. When it came to the twelfth, Den said he was determined that he would not lose the bet over a single donut. And he didn't. That's when I realized the need to water the greedy person. I haven't lost this bet since.

88

Throw a dinner party and serve an unusual delicacy (e.g., squid eggs, squirrel loins, sheeps eyes, bulls pizzle, etc.) Eat with obvious relish and encourage all your guests to do the same. If the delicacy really is so unusual as to constitute a problem, anesthetize your taste buds with a preliminary shot of neat scotch. This is the only way I can deal with those pale green stinking balls of hell, brussels sprouts.

Variant 1: The guests servings are real, but yours is only an imitation, e.g., caviar for squid eggs.

Variant 2: Every one gets a delectable morsel, but

you misidentify the food to them as a less palatable alternative.*

89

The ant is one of the most industrious creatures in the animal kingdom. But no matter how busy he is, an ant can always find the time to go to a picnic. Every ant loves to picnic, and this workaholic little critter doesn't make a big fuss about etiquette; whether you invite him or not, he'll head for your food just as fast as his six little legs can carry him.

It's an inviolable law of nature that there must be ants at a picnic. So bring some of your own, little plastic ones, to make the quota high enough that the real ones can stay away. You can cunningly position these replicas on delicacies you want to save for yourself.

Avoid the twin setbacks of chewing on one of your fake ants, and even worse, chewing on a real ant under the false impression that it's one of yours.

90

I once found myself in Death Valley, California, reputedly the hottest place in the United States. It seemed as though this would be a good place to test the old saying that it was "hot enough to fry eggs on the car hood." I pulled out a stick of butter and rubbed it on the hood. It melted at once and spread into a sticky

*Billi Gordon's delightful cook book *You've Had Worse Things in Your Mouth!* (published by West Graphics, ISBN 0-9614979-0-4) contains a chapter entitled "Revenge Cooking" dedicated to this subject. It is replete with suggestions such as preparing what appears to be scalloped potatoes stuffed with cheese, but is actually a stuffing of raw sea urchin.

Some people claim that this is in bad taste, but to me it's just tongue-in-cheek.

pool. A promising start. I broke an egg onto the fat and stood back to let it sizzle. It didn't. The white of the egg was not quite hot enough to coagulate and cook.

The problem was that my car was white, a color that reflects the largest part of ambient solar radiation (which, from a physics viewpoint, is why we perceive the color as white). A black car would have given much better results, but there are very few dark-colored cars in hot climates, precisely because they do absorb too much solar radiation and heat up unpleasantly. That's why dark-colored cars are hot and lighter cars are cool. So you should buy a black car if you want people to think you are hot, but a white one if you want them to think you are cool.

This apparent failure did not deter me from faking a successful result and having my picture taken by some impressed tourists. I told them they should have come the previous day, when I had roasted a chicken.

91

My brother-in-law Andrew is very partial to Indian food, and he used to patronize a curry house near his place of work. The restaurant staff were young and playful. This was the place where someone ordered a beer, and Andrew asked for one, too, adding, "and make sure it's in a clean glass." A couple of minutes later the waiter brought out a tray with two glasses of beer, looked at them, and asked, "Now, who wanted the clean one?"

The restaurant was actually a pleasant enough place, but one thing used to annoy Andrew; he always felt that the china plates weren't properly preheated, thus the food cooled down too quickly. Every time he ate there Andrew would complain about the cold plates, but it never seemed to make any difference.

One lunchtime, Andrew went for a curry with a group of his coworkers. They ordered the meal, Andrew made his customary plea for hotter plates, and the meal seemed to take a few minutes longer than usual to come. Then Andrew noticed that all the staff had come out of the kitchen and were glancing across at his table stifling giggles. The waiter arrived carrying a pile of plates on a tray, and motioned to Andrew to take the top one. Andrew realized at once that it had probably been cunningly preheated to about the boiling point of lead.

But Andrew is an Englishman, used to showing no emotion at all under duress. Without flinching, he firmly grasped the top plate, which was indeed scorching, and set it down in front of him without undue haste. The waiter and all the onlooking staff were completely devastated, and the rest of the meal continued as normal.

Finally the time came to pay the check and leave. There was only one possible thing to do, and Andrew did it. Pulling out a few dollars worth of change in silver coins, he heated them to an appropriate temperature with his pocket lighter and left them for the tip. They say the waiter's yelp could be heard all the way to Madras.

92

My good friend Nick played this trick on me at my last party. Nick wandered into the kitchen, where the liquor was laid out. Five minutes later he wandered out, having relabeled all the booze. The wine bottles now sported labels ranging from "Old Camel Pee" to "Vintage: Last Thursday," while the beer kegs were marked with warnings like "Old Rotgut. Maximum Dose 0.5 pints."

These labels were professionally printed, and were close facsimiles of existing trademarks. The overall effect provided a lot of laughter, but the strangest aspect was that people were not in the least detered by these detestable stickers. The lewdly labeled liquor seemed more popular than ever; perhaps people appreciated the truth in advertising.

There is also the standard St. Patrick's Day practice of dyeing the beer green. A surprising number of people find this off-putting. Green beer is completely unknown in Britain, and when I attempted to introduce the custom at a student party, the verdant brew was the only liquor untouched by the end of the evening.

93

Don't overlook the trusty old trick of slicing a banana that is still unpeeled. This is done by inserting a fine needle through the skin, and levering it from side to side. Do this at several points down the banana. It totally amazes children. Tell them you buy the presliced kind because it saves time.

94

At college, my roommates and I started a tradition of cooking wholesome and elaborate Sunday lunches. At our very first one, we discovered that we lacked a gravy boat. We substituted a teapot. The idea quickly caught on to become one of the most popular traditions of the dorm.

Dignified guests at future meals were often perplexed at the novel gravy container, but since everyone else treated it as perfectly normal, they would, too. Try it at your next dinner party.

95

It is a sad but true fact that most English people have never seen popcorn being popped. Remedy this gap in their education.

Give a packet of popcorn to someone who hasn't seen it before, and tell them to fry the contents. They won't think to put a lid on the frying pan, and just watch them jump when the corn starts popping out of the pan.

This gag works especially well because nothing happens for the first several minutes, lulling the victim into a false sense of security. Then suddenly all the corn explodes at once.

If you think Elvis is everywhere, then just wait till you see a kitchen after the popcorn gag. Be prepared to spend fifteen minutes helping the dupe pick up pieces of popcorn from the floor, walls, and ceiling.

Wedding
Wonderment

Matrimony, as they say, is not a word—it's a sentence. Those who know, say that the decision to get married is usually the last decision a man makes for himself for the rest of his life. Other people claim that a bigamist is someone who *knows* that he has one wife too many, while a monogamist merely *thinks* so.

Be that as it may, you bachelors can't go on enjoying yourselves for ever. You'll have to get married sometime. Perhaps some of the ideas here will help you to make your own or a friend's wedding a day to remember forever.

96

Attach little bells to the frame of the nuptial bed. The most suitable bells are the kind sold in pet shops for cat collars. Use wire to fasten them to the bed. About sixty-seven should be enough. Now is not the time to stint your best buddy and his new wife. If anyone in the honeymoon room so much as coughs, the bed should ring like a firehouse with a three-alarm fire.

97

When Harris got married, he wisely chose me as his best man, thus ensuring that all my energies would be devoted to preventing pranks on his behalf, not playing them. I even bribed the bellhop at the hotel not to let anyone into the matrimonial bedchamber.

Unfortunately Harris's brother-in-law paid out a bigger bribe and got into the room. In the space of about a quarter of an hour he completely dismantled the bed and hid its component parts behind and in the wardrobe. Toward the end of the celebrations, at the far end of a long and tiring day, Harris went to check on the room and was aghast to find that the bed had apparently disappeared into thin air.

Harris's eyes were bulging like a swamp frog's throat in the mating season, and I could see that he didn't intend to solve the problem with a power smile. So to forestall the imminent crisis, I paid a third bribe to the bellhop to procure a replacement bed immediately. That's life in the big city for you.

98

Harris's stag night was scheduled for the eve of his wedding, and his bride-to-be had her bridal shower on the same night. The two events contrasted greatly in refinement. In fact, the stag night was just getting started as the shower was ending. A group of us stags flagged down a cab outside the hotel, to take us to the first bar. By coincidence the cab was just dropping off the voluptuous Karen, returning from the bridal shower.

One of the stags, Charles, had never met Karen. Charles is an Englishman and fancies himself to be rather a dashing rake. He was immediately smitten with Karen and rather grandly (and presumptuously) invited her to Harris's wedding for the following day. Charles had no idea that Karen was actually an officially invited guest. For her part, Karen recognized the rest of the wedding party, secretly winked at me, and told Charles she'd come along if she had the time.

The next day immediately before the wedding, Charles, Harris, and I were waiting outside the cathedral when Karen arrived and waved rather jauntily at Charles. Charles's jaw fell to the floor, bounced on the sidewalk, and clipped a neat piece from his mustache on the way up again. He screwed up his courage (and why not, he'd screwed up everything else), and sidled up to Karen with an embarrassed idiot grin on his face. "I say, old girl," he mumbled with downcast eyes, "I was only jokin' yesterday. I don't really have any right to invite you."

Karen was too kind to let Charles squirm for long, but it was an exquisite moment, crafted through her quick thinking and perfect timing.

99

One of the best wedding spoofs is to slip on some artificial face decoration for one of the wedding pictures. I'm talking about a clown's red nose, or giant pointy "Mr. Spock" ears, or werewolf fangs. Play fair and only appear in one picture like this. If you have several like-minded colleagues, make sure that you synchronize your funning so that you all don your disguises for the same one picture.

A nice variant which allows you to appear eccentric but not totally ridiculous is to wear a stupid fish necktie. This is a tie woven to look like a fish hanging by the tail from the wearer's neck. If you think about it, a tie does have the approximate shape of a fish in profile. I have seen this tie offered for sale in the Northwest Orient Airline gift catalog in three species: striped bass, salmon, and tuna.

This prank can be applied to all kinds of official and unofficial photographs, not just wedding pictures. A man wearing the tuna variety appears in a group of staff on page 9 of the VLSI Inc. 1986 annual report. If you don't have any of the fun equipment, the last-ditch standby is simply to cross your eyes wildly as you look at the camera. Works for police lineups, too.

100

Many grooms, on getting married for the first time, forget to remove the price tag from the soles of their new shoes. As they kneel at the front of the altar, they expose their footwear budget to the assembled congregation.

A classic joke is to take advantage of this footwear forgetfulness. Chalk or paint a simple but moving message on the groom's shoes before he puts them on. Something like "Help!" or "Take me away" would be appropriate. The words should be written up by the heels of the shoes, where the sole doesn't touch the ground, and hence won't be scuffed off.

101

There is something about official church functions that brings out the worst in me. And the line in the marriage ceremony where the minister asks "if anyone knows just cause why these two people should not be joined," is nothing short of an incitement.

While I personally have always taken the option of "forever keeping my peace," I have heard the following (probably apocryphal) tale. The minister poses the question, and a gaunt and solemn man at the back of the church rises from his seat. In a deep, emotion-laden voice, he commands that the ceremony stop, for he has just reason. He slowly advances down the aisle to the front of the church, where he confronts the bride, groom, and reverend. He examines the betrothed couple carefully from head to foot, then suddenly barks, "Sorry—wrong church," and stalks out. Most women would not see the funny side of this.

102

Don't hesitate to hire the services of a "funny-person-a-gram." For the price of a magnum of champagne, you can liven up any wedding reception.

When my sister Catherine got married, a large reception was held at a nearby hall. As the assembled guests sat down to eat the wedding breakfast, a "Tarzan-a-gram" suddenly burst in. It was a tanned muscular individual dressed only in a leopard-skin loincloth, and reflective sunglasses.

"Catherine," he called out, "Catherine, how could you do this to me? First Jane, and now you!" Then he ran the length of the room and swept the bride off her feet, posed for a couple of pictures, beat his chest for a Tarzan yodel, and left as quickly as he had arrived.

Cath's husband is a policeman, and he and all his detective friends were completely baffled. The guests were vastly bemused, and the ushers were dumbfounded. But nobody was more surprised than I; for, you see, I had specified a gorilla when I placed the order.

103

My colleague Jim, who is to bachelorhood what Lassie is to dog meat, has on occasion expressed his idea of the perfect wedding ceremony. It features himself as the groom and the front pews filled with six voluptuous, heartbroken, sobbing, beautiful women. Jim explains that he has remained a bachelor up till now because "Saying yes to one woman is saying no to millions; many of whom I have not yet dated. . . ."

Jim recently announced a change of heart. He plans to marry in the spring. You can just bet that a small circle of Jim's friends will be doing everything we can to make Jim's fantasy come true. At least he didn't specify virgins. Gorgeous women we can probably manage, but where would we find six virgins in New Jersey?

Phone Fun

Phone "phreaking" is a pastime that became both popular and notorious a few years ago. Phone phreaks were people who had a detailed technical knowledge of the phone network and could use their skills to avoid paying for calls or to otherwise subvert the system.

Under the R1 telephone signaling system used in North America, a call is routed to its destination by multifrequency tones sent in the voice channel. This is the series of fast beeps you sometimes hear after dialing a long-distance call, before the ringing starts. It's easy for electronics engineers to build "blue boxes" and place their own signaling tones on the line. A "blue box" is merely a frequency generator held up to the phone mouthpiece. By making the right tone sounds, a person can divert a call charged at local rates onto the out-of-state or international network.

Simpler still is the "Captain Crunch toy whistle," which for a time came free in boxes of breakfast cereal. By chance, the whistle generated a 2600Hz tone—the same as used in R1 call setup. If you made a long-distance call and blew the whistle before the call completed, the tone caused the distant exchange to release (drop the call, but keep the line). When the 2600Hz tone stopped (because you stopped blowing the whistle), the distant exchange would recognize a new call attempt and prepare for digit reception. A phone phreak could then dial a new long-distance number to call. Meanwhile the call-initiating end (the end where you are standing with your whistle) had no knowledge of any of this activity and would continue billing as though the call to the original number was continuing. John

Draper, who took on the name "Captain Crunch," became famous by discovering this anomaly.

The phone company was alerted when some phreaks got too greedy and started placing their setup calls to toll-free numbers such as army recruiting offices. Nobody, not even Rambo, talks to army recruiting for two hours. When such calls started showing up regularly, it was obvious that something was amiss.

Captain Crunch phone phreaking seems too good a story to be true, but I can definitely vouch for its accuracy. Another popular tale holds that some blind people, gifted with perfect pitch, have learned to whistle the right tone combinations. It's a nice story, and maybe there really are people who can whistle multiple tones simultaneously.

Phone phreaking, while interesting, is illegal. Anyway it will all stop with Number 7 signaling, which is gradually replacing the R1 protocol. But don't despair, as there are plenty of amusing pranks that can legitimately be played with the aid of the telephone. Don't overplay any of these phone frolics as they quickly lose their novelty. About one gag per person per year is adequate for most situations.

The only other fact you need to know is why phone booths always smell like somebody peed in them. Nine times out of ten it is because somebody did. The tenth phone booth is brand-new from the factory, where the final stage in manufacturing is to apply this odor. The phone company orders them like this to encourage you to keep your calls short.

104

Try getting two people on the phone, each of whom believes the other placed the call. This can be done on any phone connected to a Number 5 telephone exchange with the "Centrex" features. Most modern office-phone systems have this capability. If your phone allows you to create three-party "conference calls," you can do it. Dial the first party, and while the phone is ringing, hook-flash (momentarily press then release the switch on which the phone handset normally rests). The phone will give another dial tone, so you can dial the second party. You now have two phones ringing and connected to your phone. Stay on the line to listen to the fun, which will go something like this:

First Party: "Hello?"
Second Party: "Hello, yes?"
First Party: "Yes, go ahead."
Second Party: "Who's calling please?"
First Party: "Sprouts here, can I help you?"
Second Party: "Turnip speaking. Who do you want?"
First Party: "I don't want anyone. What do *you* want?"
Second Party: "It's not my call, it's yours!"
First Party: "I didn't make this call, Turnip, you idiot, you did!"
Second Party: "Call to say I'm an idiot, would you, Sprouts?"
etc. etc.

Even without a Centrex office-phone system, you can play this trick. Simply dial the two parties from two adjacent phones (for example, two public phone booths). Tape the two handsets together, so that the mouthpiece of the first is next to the earpiece of the second and vice versa. And for those who like their vice versa, this is called "sixty-nining the phones" in telecommunication parlance.

In general, it's a good plan to connect together two parties with a common interest (for instance mutual hatred of each other). And if you like the effect with two parties, try it with three or four.

105

The very best practical jokes work by creating a completely unexpected effect with an everyday object. A classic prank of this type is to fix a phone so that it continues to ring even after the victim picks it up.

There are several ways of doing this, and they all involve fixing the hook switch (the cradle on which the phone handset normally rests), so that it does not detect the handset has been picked up. The phone thus continues to ring. The easiest method is to use clear tape to tape the switch down. Lay the tape so that the victim won't feel it when picking up the phone handset. A more subtle but complicated variant is to remove the cover from the phone and adjust the inside of the off-hook switch. This would be appropriate when funning a rocket scientist.

Go to another nearby phone and dial the victim's number. The phone will continue ringing after it is answered, leading to maximal confusion for the victim, and amusement for all other parties.

106

The musically inclined can use the numbers on a touch-tone* phone to play little tunes to the person on the other end. Dial the number you want, and after the other party answers, use the tone dial like a piano keyboard. The tones used by the Bell touch-tone system are:

*"Touch-tone" is a registered trademark of Bell Telephone. Whoop-de-do.

Phone key	Tones
1	697Hz and 1209Hz
2	697Hz and 1336Hz
3	697Hz and 1477Hz
4	770Hz and 1209Hz
5	770Hz and 1336Hz
6	770Hz and 1477Hz
7	852Hz and 1209Hz
8	852Hz and 1336Hz
9	852Hz and 1477Hz
*	941Hz and 1209Hz
0	941Hz and 1336Hz
#	941Hz and 1477Hz

The R2 signaling system tones, used in Europe, are a little different but approximate to these frequencies. Harris reports that the tones ring true in Hong Kong, too.

It would be a bit problematic to pick out a tune, because as the table above shows, all of the keys generate our old friend the multifrequency tone. But by good fortune (good-for-tune?) on most touch-tone phones, pressing two keys at once causes only the common tone to sound. Although your fingers play a chord, you only get a single note. Mike, my saxophone instructor with near-perfect pitch, identified the following notes:

Phone keys	Frequency	Musical Note
1 & 3	697Hz	flat F
4 & 6	770Hz	G-flat
7 & 9	852Hz	A-flat
* & #	941Hz	B-flat
7 & 1	1209Hz	high D-sharp
8 & 2	1336Hz	high E
9 & 3	1477Hz	high F-sharp

These are the only notes that can be generated, and they can all be generated by several different key pairs. The notes are deliberately rather strange, because the frequencies were chosen so that they have no harmonics in common. While these notes don't form a scale, they are enough to play some simple tunes. "Happy Birthday" for example is:

Hap—py   Birth—day to   you,
1&3   1&3 4&6   1&3 *&# 7&9

Hap—py   Birth—day to   you,
1&3   1&3 4&6   1&3 7&1 *&#

Hap—py   Birth—day dear Pump—kin
1&3   1&3 7&1   *&#*&#7&9   4&6

Hap—py   Birth—day to   you.
1&7   1&7 *&#   4&6 7&9 4&6

and "Swing Low, Sweet Chariot" is:

Swinglow, sweetcha   —ri —o   —t
7&1   *&# 7&1   *&# *&# 4&6 1&3

Co   —min'for to   car —ry me home
*&# *&#   *&#*&# 7&1 7&1 7&1 9&3

The secret to playing well is to practice first. Other good tunes: "Pennsylvania 6–5000," "The Wichita Lineman," Blondie's "Call Me," or "Hanging on the Telephone," etc.

107

Anyone who owns a telephone answering machine has great potential for extra humor. This can be in the form of the message you record for your callers. Novelty messages have come to be so popular that you can even buy a range of prerecorded funny answering cassettes from Radio Shack ("celebrity voices," musical accompaniments, etc). One splendid recording sonorously intones "there's no-bo-dy home" to the opening bars of Beethoven's Fifth Symphony. One of my colleagues, I'll call him Jim here (because that's his name), prefers to develop his own novelties.

One of Jim's best was the "KGB ploy," in which his answering machine talks to you as "comrade" and announces in a thick Russian accent that the party chairman is currently out bringing capitalism to its knees. It ends with the request to "please leave your name and number, though you really don't need to as we are already watching you and know who you are. . . ."

If your callers are alert, they can deliver a boomerang by leaving you a novelty response. For example, they could pretend that your message is a real person ("Broccoli, I know that's you. I can hear you breathing"), or complain about the volume or the cheesy tone ("Call that a message tone? Get yourself a proper tone, and I'll leave a message"). There are countless variations on this theme, and a whole book* has been published giving smartass retorts to answering machines.

108

I used to have a perfectly sensible recorded message in Chinese on my answering machine, but too many of my friends started leaving messages also in Chinese (they would call from the office with a native Chinese speaker standing by). I then switched to a recording of the busy signal. That fooled too many people, so I

---

*The book is *Getting Even with the Answering Machine* by John Carfi and Cliff Carle, published by CCC Publications, ISBN 0-918259-01-0. It contains many ideas like the ingenious message: "This is the Specialty Livestock Corp. Our delivery van was in an accident today, and 5000 of our laboratory fleas escaped onto your property. After due consideration we have decided you can keep them."

switched to a recording that said in an official-sounding recorded voice, "You have reached 624-4377. That number has been changed to 624-4377."

Some people never realized that if they just stayed on the line the tone would sound and they could leave a message. They would try calling the perfectly correct number over and over.

The golden palm for originality and abuse goes to my colleague Celerytop, whose shtick went as follows:

[Celerytop's machine]
"Hello, this is Celerytop. I've decided I don't want to talk to you now, but you can leave a message if you want."

[silence]
You: "Very funny Celerytop, I was calling to—"

[Celerytop's machine]
"Not now dummy, wait for the tone!"

109

An old chestnut of a prank, which has been around for hundreds of millions of years last Tuesday, since even before Diana Dors roamed the earth, is the "fake phone engineer" stunt. The basic ploy is to phone an unsuspecting dupe, persuade him that you are a phone maintenance engineer, and talk him into doing some unlikely act under the pretext that it will help trace a phone fault.

Some popular acts in the past have been: backing away from the phone while whistling or singing; hanging the phone out of the window; putting the phone under the desk while standing on the desk and shouting ("the desk acts as a sounding board, you see, to test those low frequencies"). This will only work on someone who can be outwitted by a tuna fish. A tuna fish that is still in the can.

Advise credulous customers to put some covering over the phone for the next hour. Inform them that the phone company will be blowing high-pressure air down the lines to clear away accumulated dust. Explain that the phone company cannot be responsible for dust and dirt coming into the room from an uncovered phone. Zinger: Sometime in the next hour secretly sneak a little dust from the vacuum cleaner around the phone. The recipient will accept this as expected, leaving the door open for even wilder spoofs (underwater-cable flushing perhaps) in future.

The ploy requires the bogus engineer to have the acting talent of an Oliver. Since most of us are more at the Sylvester Stallone or Marlon Brando level, it is probably not so hot an idea for the novice prankster.

110

When people answer the phone, they usually expect the caller to be someone they know, or at least someone with a good reason for calling. There are several kinds of strange calls that you can transfer to a poor unsuspecting dupe, which will be totally unexpected. If you are using an office phone, you should transfer the call so that it appears to be a regular incoming call on the victim's line.

The telephone service in London offers a daily leisure line promoting local tourist events. Different numbers offer the forecast in different languages. I generally find the report in German provides good results for non-German speakers. Bonus points are awarded the longer it takes the victim to realize he is connected to a recording.

111

Another popular modern phone service is the "dial-a-pillow talk," where a real live woman will perform aural sex (i.e., she'll talk dirty into your ear—I'm not making this up) on receipt of $25 from your credit card. If this isn't a "hot line," I don't know what is. The phone numbers are available in the back pages of any medium-strength men's magazine (*Buns 'n Bimbos*, for example). If you are too cheap to spring 25 bucks to really surprise your buddy, then several of these services offer a free sample (by recorded message) and you can choose one of these. Alternatively, raise the moral tone in your neighborhood by connecting your friend to a "dial-a-children's story" or "dial-a-prayer."

112

Last and definitely least, liberally smear the earpiece of a phone with shaving cream. Then go next door and dial the number of the cream-smeared phone. You're only young once. Don't pull this one too frequently if you plan on reaching your old age.

Bedtime
Stories

If you turned to this chapter first, then this is definitely a good book that you should buy now. However, the information you are seeking is in the chapter entitled "Totally Disgusting."

The average person spends over one-third of his or her life in bed. Given the choice, I would spend my one-third on the teenage years, early middle age, and the whole of 1991 (on the basis that the only palindromic year this century ought to be marked in some special way). But Man cannot live by bed alone, so relieve the tedium with some of these pranks.

113

Here's a trick that is so venerable, it should probably be canonized. In the United States, it's known as short-sheeting the bed, and in Britain it's called making an apple-pie bed. The Italians refer to it as "sacco." The German sense of humor does not extend to this kind of pillow fun. I once asked my German pal Gemüse about the German variety of short-sheeting. He became very quiet, as though I had suggested destruction-testing a Porsche, and after some reflection replied that jovial young men would sometimes balance a liter jug of ice-cold water halfway down a newly married couple's bed. Gemüse called this a "Geschwindigheitbegrenzungarbeitslosstrudelspiel," or in English, "bed joke." The French don't play any of these sort of tricks in bed.

Short-sheeting consists of folding the top sheet on a bed back on itself halfway down the bed. The pillow is placed between the top and bottom parts of the top sheet. The bed looks like a normally made bed, but anyone getting into it will discover that, because the sheet loops back to be both under and over them, they can only get their legs about halfway down.

This will cause strained muscles for you and endless laughter for your great-grandfather, who probably played the same trick on Noah. The only cure for a short-sheeted bed is to get up and remake it. Then retaliate the following night with one of the other ruses given here.

114

Stuff your victim's bed pillow with anything hard that comes to hand. Baseball bats, shoes, toy cars, bricks, old bones, and household tools are all suitable. Confine your stuffing to the pillow underside so it doesn't show. Older brothers get real vicious about this. They will chase you for at least twenty minutes, so have your running shoes ready. If you play this trick more than three times in one year, your victim will for the rest of his life pound the pillow before laying his head on it.

115

There's nothing worse than a bed with soaking wet sheets, as the man who crossed the Mafia in the film *The Godfather* can attest. This prank relies on the victim relaxing his guard through repetition to achieve its effect.

For three successive nights you place a hot-water bottle full of cold water in your victim's bed. Each night the victim sticks his hand down between the sheets and pulls out the icy flask. On the fourth night, you seal up the bottle with a cork tied to the foot of the bed. When your victim thoughtlessly tugs up the flask, the cork stays put and he leaves a trail of cold water through his bed.

116

One year at summer camp, it became a favorite nocturnal joke to silently remove a bed and its slumbering occupant to outside the bunk. Pleased with their initial success, the pranksters became more ambitious, and the next night relocated a bed to the middle of the sports field. It is necessary to drape a sheet from the head to the foot of the bed to insulate the occupant from any temperature or light changes. Five or six people can easily move a bed and sleeper with the minimum of disturbance.

The joke got out of hand as more people wanted to try it. Two or three beds were traveling each night to places farther and farther away. People were trying hard not to fall asleep first, and were going to bed with their clothes and money for bus tickets to minimize the inconvenience of return.

One camper wired his bed to the floor. It took me about two seconds to cut through the wires. I unscrewed the legs from my own bed. When rival jokesters picked up the bed frame, the legs fell to the floor with a clatter and roused me.

117

Few things encourage a man to work harder than the knowledge that his boss is working equally as energetically. That's why it was so distressing for me to work in a large oil company where my boss spent most afternoons literally asleep at his desk. We had a large openplan office, and he occupied one corner opposite the corridor to the elevator. Every afternoon at five P.M. he would be awakened by the sounds of the mass exodus from work.

The situation plainly called for me to do something, but what exactly? One day, my lazy leader came back to the office after a particularly heavy liquid lunch and rapidly fell into his usual deep slumber. I seized my chance and started moving partitions around. I walled him in completely and rerouted the exit corridor so that it ran down the far wall.

That evening we all went home while the boss snored on. He was discovered hours later by the cleaners, in an otherwise deserted office. Undisturbed, he had slumbered on. (Note from Copy Editor: This is the funniest practical joke I have ever heard, and I laughed till the tears ran over my desk, smudging the ink on this manuscript.) (Note from Publisher: You're weird and you're fired.)

118

I have a small alarm clock, made by Braun in West Germany. It has a conventional "snooze" control, allowing you to defer the wake-up alarm for an extra five minutes, with one unusual feature: it is voice-activated.

It is quite a bit simpler than this seems at first sight. There is a microphone in the face of the clock that will react to any loud sound (a voice or a handclap) once the alarm has started. If the microphone picks up any input, it will stop the alarm and switch it on again five minutes later. That is the only level of control you have over it. Nonetheless, this simple clock has afforded me endless amusement.

The key idea is to convince your sleeping partner that the clock has a lot more intelligence than it actually does. You start one evening by secretly setting the alarm for the usual time in the morning. After you have both gotten into bed, you pretend to have forgotten to set it. "But never mind," you say, "the clock responds to spoken commands." You call out a clear instruction to the clock: "*Clock! Set your alarm for 7:35 A.M.*" Your partner will assume you are having brain fade, then you both go to sleep.

The next morning, the alarm goes off as instructed. You yawn and, mentioning that you could use another five minutes sleep, call out a five-minute "snooze" command to the clock: "*Clock! give me a five-minute snooze period, starting NOW!*" The microphone picks up the noise and goes into snooze mode. Five minutes later the alarm rings again. You instruct the clock to switch itself off: "*Clock! Deactivate alarm.*" Hearing the noise it again goes into snooze mode to defer the alarm by five minutes. You get out of bed, and while puttering around (perhaps moving it from the bureau to the dresser), actually switch it off before the five minutes have elapsed.

After a couple of days like this, you will have convinced your partner that the clock is at least as intelligent as most state senators, and a whole lot more useful. From there, you can get as fancy as you want. Encouraging your partner to switch it off herself vocally is a good first step. Women exhibit a strange and unnatural reluctance to talk to alarm clocks, but with patience and care you can achieve wonders. Then you can build up to getting her to set it vocally, sustaining the illusion of spoken control by some fancy sleight of hand.

If the relationship comes to an end, give the clock to your ex-partner. The whole fruitless performance will provide an entertaining spectacle for her next official stud.

If you turned to this chapter first, then this is definitely the book for you. If you don't care to use it directly, then buy it for your brother-in-law's children. He'll probably never speak to you again.

I never bear anyone a grudge, any longer than absolutely necessary. And on the occasions when it is necessary, a selection from this chapter may be helpful.

119

Cover the toilet seat with Vaseline. Your friends will slither everywhere, in a most interesting manner. Or lightly smear the phone receiver with Vaseline. This is also a good way for parents to give themselves some privacy in the bedroom; smear the outside of the bedroom doorknob with Vaseline. Little children may be able to reach it, but they sure can't turn it.

Finally profit from the example of the newlywed couple who didn't know the difference between Vaseline and putty. Yes, it's true; all their windows fell out.

120

An old navy trick is to disgust new recruits by the following ploy. A sailor conceals a piece of peeled grape (or mushroom or clam) in his palm. This material looks rather like something that might have originated in his nose or throat. The sailor then pretends to sneeze into his hand, and wipes the fragment onto the tablecloth.

The surrounding new recruits are disgusted; some of them think it's funny, other'snot. Zinger: A second sailor, in on the joke, seizes the grape fragment and swallows it. Boomerang: the first sailor then opens his hand to the second sailor, revealing the grape remnant still in his palm. . . .

121

Condoms are made in two standard lengths: 150–170 millimeters, and 170–190 millimeters. The size is rarely shown on the packet, but drugstores seldom allow the customer to try the goods for fit before purchase. Either size is said to fit all, but those who know, warn that if you are used to the larger size and suddenly switch to the smaller one, it will bring a tear to your eye. Without getting into an unnecessary level of detail, the problem is not the length but the diameter. Either size is suitable for all condom capers.

Slip a condom under a victim's door. Fill it to capacity* with water from a hose and knot the end. It will swell up nearly to the size of an oil drum. If the door is opened carelessly or the condom is manhandled, it will burst. It is sporting to warn the victim.

Should you ever find yourself the recipient of this antic, the best way to remove the swollen rubber is to push it and roll it to a place where it may be safely burst. Like your enemy's bedroom.

---

*The scientifically inclined will be pleased to learn that there is an international standard for the strength and leakage of condoms. The United States, Britain, and Japan all use the tensile-strength test. A strip of condom material must be stretchable to 7.5 times its size, and must withstand a pressure of 240kg force per square centimeter.

These specifications usually exceed the operational requirements for normal deployment. In Britain, condoms are made in compliance with British Standard 3704; but then again, so was the S.S. *Titanic*.

122

Inflate a condom like a balloon and bounce it into the air. The textured condom variety ("with knobs on") seems to exhibit particularly good flight characteristics. A pop concert is a most acceptable venue. When the teenagers start to shriek and flinch hysterically, you can gain bonus points by stating the obvious ("It's only a condom for goodness' sake, it won't hurt you") in an authoritative voice.

123

In winter, build some realistically erotic snowmen and snowwomen in your yard. Depending on your skill as an artist you might want to confine your snow exhibitionism to the backyard. You should only use artificial props (carrots, coal, etc.) for facial features.

If you build one of the snowmen on a board, then each evening you can slide it nearer to the snowwomen. See how far things can go before the spring thaw sets in. It brings a whole new dimension to the term *snowball fight*.

124

There is an elegant bronze statue of General Lafayette mounted on horseback in the center of the city of Hartford, Connecticut. The members of a fraternity of Trinity University have a standard gag of polishing the horse's scrotum to an eye-catching gleam. The rest of the statue is a dull gray-green color, and the gleaming golden balls, therefore, stand out in a rather obvious way.

This prank is the exact reverse of vandalism. In contrast to painting something on the horse, the gag merely restores something to its original state, and so it would presumably be very difficult for the authorities to press a complaint. The idea could be extended to the applying of slogans by sandblasting clean patches of letters onto a dirty graffiti-covered wall.

125

Place Mr. Cling Film over Mr. Toilet Bowl. Yes, this is extremely childish and scatological. Adults will immediately form a posse and hunt you down like the pond scum you are. But remember the golden rule: better retaliate than never.

Everyone is entitled to play this joke no more than once in their lifetime. This gag often brings on profound thoughtfulness in its victim. Thoughtfulness directed wholly toward the suspected prankster and what might befall him in the future.

126

This trick is disgusting, not in its effect but in its treachery. It was a prank that Harris came upon quite spontaneously, and almost by accident. He was enjoying a lunchtime meal with two office buddies in a local bar. The three of them ordered low-alcohol beer to accompany the meal. A short while later, a fourth friend joined them, saw they were drinking "beer," and ordered a Carlsberg. An evil glint came into Harris's beady eyes.

After a while, when the glasses were nearing the low-water mark, Harris beckoned the waiter, ordered a Carlsberg, and "same again." Later, one of the other colleagues ordered "same again." And then finally so did the last colleague. Harris reports that it was a very amusing lunch, made more so by the unwitting assistance of the waiter and of course the victim, who was merrily pickling himself under the totally unfounded assumption that there was safety in numbers.

Incidentally, it's an alarmingly educational experience to sit sober with someone who is becoming intoxicated. You notice the difference after just one glass. It causes a terrible feeling of "déjà bu" (already drunk).

127

This practical joke takes a bit of setting up, but is worth it for the effect it produces. I don't have any personal experience, but I can believe it is really effective.

Fit a microswitch to a lavatory seat and use this to control a cassette recorder. Record an appropriate message so that when the victim sits on the pan, a shout apparently blares up from the bowl: "Yo! Hold it, buddy. Whaddya think you're doin'? There's plumbers working down here!"

I don't know why, but a Bronx accent seems to fit in best here.

128

Dipping a sleeper's hand in a bowl of warm water is said to make him wet the bed. I have not tested this personally, but unscrupulous colleagues assure me that it is true.

129

One prank which occurs repeatedly in American folklore is the "shit-kicking fire-stomping grocery bag." The jester scoops a helping of horse manure into a brown paper grocery bag and folds the top over. The bag is then placed on someone's doorstep, and lit so that it smolders. Ring the doorbell and shout "fire." The house-holder will come running out and stamp on the bag or kick it off the doorstep. Either way, he is fairly certain to get bespattered with the horse manure.

This prank isn't really worth beans, but it is so widely known that it needs to be cataloged here. The modern artist Lowell Darling, who ran for governor of California in 1978, describes how, when he was a boy, he played this trick with another rascal. As they leaped a hedge to run away, his friend had a heart attack and fell down dead. Let that be a lesson to us all.

130

If you have access to a Jacuzzi, then try to convince a visiting friend that the "house rules" specify nakedness (maybe your house rules already do, in which case try to convince your friend that the house rules specify wearing a life belt). Set up your friend by secretly donning two swimsuits. Enter the Jacuzzi, switch it on, and then explain the house rule while removing only one of your two swimsuits. Fling it out of reach, and put the peer-group pressure on your erstwhile buddy to do likewise. It really helps to have a couple of nubile bimbettes on hand, who are in on the joke and do the same as you.

With all the foaming and thrashing of the water jets, your buddy will be unable to see that you have, once more, fitted him up. Until the music stops, that is, when the size of his predicament will be clear (so to speak).

131

My good friend Nick is a womanizer in the same sense that the Hoover dam is a "river obstruction."

Many people consider him an authority on women; the women might not know about him, but the authorities certainly do. At Manchester University, students would sometimes sprain an ankle or shoulder playing strenuous sports. But not Nick. After an evening touring the city bars, Nick injured his ankle trying to climb over a wall into the girls' dorm.

Last year, around his birthday, Nick appeared rather tired. Diagnosing the most likely cause, I decided to make him a present of a battery-operated vibrator (the "Sailorboy maximus joy plus" model, with variable three speeds, dual control, and autopilot).

We were celebrating his birthday in a crowded bar and attracting a certain amount of attention. As a general principle, any mechanical toy should always be handed to the recipient wrapped up but switched on and operating. Seizing the opportunity I switched the implement on (I nearly wrote "turned it on"), resealed the wrapping paper, and handed the shaking buzzing package to him.

As soon as Nick felt the package throbbing and pulsating in his hands he knew what it was. Nick has always been a man to rise to the occasion, and this time was no exception. He unwrapped the vibrating dildo, brandished it at the crowd, and turned to thank me. "Peter," he said simply, "wherever I use this, I will think of you."

"Wherever"? Yeah, right. Thanks, Nick.

Party
Time

Have you ever wondered why people throw parties? Me neither. But if you enjoy parties as much as I do, you are probably reading this from a hospital bed right now.

Over the years, I have developed a kind of Richter scale of party enjoyment; instead of measuring earthquake intensity, it measures party intensity. The highest point on the real Richter scale is characterized by the description "objects are thrown violently upward into the air," and by a happy chance this coincides exactly with the highest reading on my party Richter scale. For the dedicated party animal the other readings are:

Intensity Characteristic Events

1.   Guests arrive by limousine. Early arrivals are playing eight-ball pool. Guests compliment you on your lamp shades.

2.   Early arrivals are looking for empty bedrooms. Latecomers are parking on your neighbor's lawn. An emergency trip to the liquor store takes place. Lamp shades are knocked over.

3.   Departing guests abandon their cars, but can't remember their home address for the cabdriver. Guests are wearing lamp shades on their heads. Some people are juggling with balls from the pool table. The police arrive but can't find anyone coherent enough to point out the host. The liquor store has barricaded its doors shut.

Intensity Characteristic Events

4.   Guests who can still stand are attempting
            to swing around the room on the chande-
            liers. A plume of smoke is drifting up from
            the rubble of the liquor store. Cabdrivers
            tell their dispatchers to ignore all calls
            from this side of town. The policemen
            who arrived earlier are now on the roof laugh-
            ing crazily and hurling balls from the pool
            table at passing airliners.

The scale extends even higher, but those who can
remember what happened generally refuse to testify,
and take the Fifth instead (or at least 750ml of
it).

Most of the party ideas below measure two to three
on the party intensity scale, and come with my personal
seal of approval. Satisfaction not included. Actual mile-
age guaranteed. Your batteries may vary.

132

Use superglue to bond your victim's drink to the bar
or table. This is quite easy; only a drop or two is
required when the victim is not looking. If the glue
doesn't stick, then nobody is any the wiser. This trick
works best when the drinks have been flowing for a
while.

You might as well use superglue for tricks like this,
because as everyone knows, it's completely useless for
conventional gluing jobs. Its major strength seems to be
in bonding the fingers of the user. But let's face it,
they wouldn't sell many tubes if they advertised it for
that.

133

Here's a novel idea for a party held outside or on a patio. Suspend some balloons overhead in a net or by other means. Fill a few of the balloons with, not air, but water. By the end of the evening some quiche-eater will start popping them for sure.

A variant is to fill the balloons with flour or talcum powder instead of water. Fill the balloon using a funnel, and then inflate as normal. Watch out for "blowback" during this procedure.

134

The "Vicars and Tarts" costume party is a popular English college event. The women dress up as hookers, and the men dress up as priests. It is supposed to provide each sex a chance to see the other the way they fantasize about them. There is always some glandularly overactive extrovert man who dresses as a hooker. Vicars and Tarts parties are the graduate-student equivalent of undergraduate beer bashes.

At the last Vicars and Tarts party I went to, in Manchester, England, I tried to procure a genuine hooker to accompany me. I felt it would bring the right degree of authenticity to the evening and liven the place up a bit. My plan was to put the tart before the hors d'oeuvres. I opened negotiations with a suitable call girl. She was receptive to the idea in principle, but wanted compensation for loss of an evening's earnings. Which was a tidy sum. In fact the sum was so tidy, it was positively neat. I pointed out the social advantages of the evening, but she complained and grumbled about the loss of money. She grumbled so much that I decided to abandon my plan. I suppose you could say that I actually ended up "putting the carp before the whores."

135

Throw a "Primate Party." Invite your friends to come dressed as the ape, monkey, baboon, mandrill, gorilla, orangutan, colobus, chimp, primate, gibbon, and so on, of their choice. Tell them that animal behavior will be strongly encouraged. Provide suitable refreshments: fresh fruit salad, vine juice, nuts, etc.

Alternatively, let the invitation specify a more varied range of wild animals. When all your friends arrive dressed as a traveling menagerie, they find you wearing the uniform of a zoo keeper, complete with peaked cap, leather riding boots, and whip.

136

Arrange a "Stupid T-shirt Party." This is best held as an adjunct to a summer barbecue. One of the compelling advantages of a Stupid T-shirt Party is that nobody has trouble finding suitable clothing.

There is an amazing variety of stupid T-shirts. You can see many of these any sunny day in public, and some favorites are:

- a trompe l'oeil fake shirt with a collar, tie, and pocket handkerchief. The most elaborate is the sailor's uniform, which is effective when worn with white shorts and a cap.

- a "hairy chest" T-shirt (make this one yourself using glue and any brown fibrous material). Very effective on a woman.

- a "picture of your own face" T-shirt. I got mine on top of the World Trade Center, New York City. I'm still wondering why.

- the "skeleton bones" T-shirt, which is printed with all the bones in the chest and back.

- a matched pair, where the girl wears a T-shirt saying "I'm his sister" and the guy has one proclaiming "I'm her brother."

My favorite stupid T-shirt is the one I have with a black and white line drawing of Albert Einstein poking his tongue out. The tongue has been colored deep red, like the Rolling Stones logo. My favorite intelligent T-shirt is the one that reads

> I am a tourist.
> I do not live here.
> Thank God.

Mildly insult the natives by wearing it any place in love with itself (such as New York City) or anywhere chic (such as Paris, Berlin, or San Francisco).

Other folk are fond of the space-age variant

> My mom and dad went to Alpha Centauri
> and all I got was this dumb T-shirt!

137

Try a "Bring-an-unusual-object Party." Award a special low-value booby prize for anyone claiming their partner is the unusual object. Some good "unusual objects" I have seen include: a Haitian voodoo doll, a rhino-hide bullwhip, a live tarantula spider in a jar, a glass eye (the owner had several "party tricks" with this one, including the "I've got my eye on you," and "I'll keep an eye out for you," together with appropriate actions), a Rolls-Royce winged-lady ornament, and a case of champagne. This last is maybe not so unusual, but it is ideal for a party.

138

Hold an "Out-of-season Party." Shuck off winter blues by arranging an Hawaiian party in the middle of February. Hold the party indoors and crank the heat way up. Everyone should come dressed for the beach, and the party decorations should match.

Try a St. Patrick's Day party at Halloween, or the other way around. Buy the appropriate decorations at a discount right after the real day, and store them for seven months.

139

Give a "Fetish Party." Everyone should come exhibiting their secret fetish. This allows real scope for the imagination and lets people be as wild as they like.

At the last Fetish Party I attended, I wore a false long nose and a dirty raincoat. My party piece was leaning forward to drink a beer and inserting my (false) nose into the glass instead of raising it to my lips. For some reason this brought the house down.

140

At college, Harris and I decided to throw a party and were casting around for an inspired theme. Someone mentioned that the chosen day was the birthday of a girl he knew back home and hadn't seen for a year or two. Perfect! We adopted her name and age, billing the event as "Pauline Scratton's Twenty-first Birthday Party."

We had special invitations printed, and as a zinger mailed one to Pauline. Just imagine how it feels to be invited to your own birthday party, by two people you've never heard of, in a town you've never visited. We actually got boomeranged on this, when her reply came back saying she couldn't make it as she had a party of her own to attend that night, but could we just forward the gifts. Incidentally, of all the friends we invited, not a single one asked who Pauline was. Student parties, they are truly incomparable.

141

Also at college, try a "Freshers Party." You wait for a new college year to start, with lots of impressionable freshmen, choose the group with the best living accommodations, and post notices of a party there. Do it in the first day or two (no longer) of the semester, and each of them assumes you live there or have some other right to throw a party.

It certainly cuts down on the cleaning up you have to do afterward. It is only polite to let them invite a few of their own friends.

142

My distinguished and serious friend Asparagus holds an annual "Titanic Party" every April 15 to commemorate the anniversary of the sinking of the S.S. *Titanic*. Asparagus says that when the *Titanic* sank in 1912, Western civilization went down with it. My own view is that the demise of Occidental culture dates from 1948, when the organizers of the Miss World Pageant banned animal acts. Nevermore will we witness the wonders of "Giggling Gayle and the galloping giraffes" or "Pouting Paula and her pounding puma." And you can just bet that the world is a poorer place without them.

Asparagus always orders a large bowl of punch as a table centerpiece for the Titanic dinner party. The punch has a massive chunk of ice floating in it to keep it cool, and some claim it represents the iceberg. Toward the climax of the last Titanic Party, I covertly launched a scale model of the vessel into the punch. Asparagus was well into his speech when he noticed it, and it riveted his attention. As his speech faltered, so everyone turned to look at the ship floating blithely on.

I had drilled holes in the bottom of the hull so the craft would slowly and realistically become waterlogged and sink. I can report that the dance band was not playing "Nearer My God to Thee," but rather "Girls Just Wanna Have Fun" this time around.

143

Perhaps the nicest party of all is the "Secret Santa Party." You put the names of all the participants in a hat, and each person secretly buys and wraps a gift for the person whose name they draw.

The gifts are labeled with the name of the recipient, but not the donor. The zinger is that as anonymous donors, people tend to buy much more risqué gifts than they ordinarily might. Such articles as split-crotch panties, edible underwear, vibrators, Chinese "love eggs," French ticklers, Dutch "finger-in-the-dyke" kits, instruction manuals, pillow books, leather accessories, rubberwear, etc., crop up with far more frequency than you usually see at Christmas.

144

Practical jokers also have a good chance to throw a special curved ball of their own. The last Secret Santa

Party I went to was an office Christmas party. I drew the name of one of the engineers and purchased a small gift, then for good measure threw in a bumper sticker reading "My other car is a piece of junk, too." I had no idea if he even had two cars, but it seemed too good an opportunity to miss. Finally I wrapped the parcel in a box, but glued a long protruding tube on the side, exactly as if a saucepan were wrapped up.

The poor victim was struck dumb with tingling anticipation when Santa handed him this uniquely shaped parcel. His hands trembled gleefully as he pulled the wrapping off the "handle" to reveal—a hollow tube containing a clothespin I had put there to add weight and credibility to the shape. The coupe de grâce was the bumper sticker. "But it's not true," he whined piteously. "My other car is quite good really. . . ." Merry Christmas.

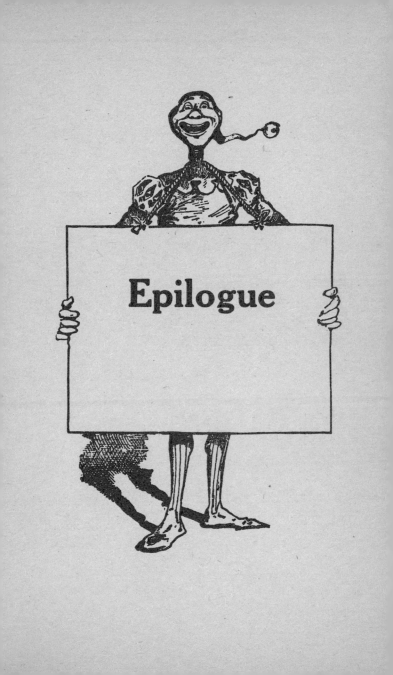

Epilogue

The author invites readers to send in descriptions of their own favorite practical jokes. The first sender of each prank selected for inclusion in a future edition will receive a free copy of that edition, together with a full acknowledgment therein.

Pranks will be judged on:

> humorous potential,
> simplicity,
> whether or not a professor is featured,
> number of free books already given away.

Send your pranks to Peter van der Linden, c/o the publisher.

183

There's an epidemic with 27 million victims. And no visible symptoms.

It's an epidemic of people who can't read.

Believe it or not, 27 million Americans are functionally illiterate, about one adult in five.

The solution to this problem is you... when you join the fight against illiteracy. So call the Coalition for Literacy at toll-free **1-800-228-8813** and volunteer.

Volunteer Against Illiteracy. The only degree you need is a degree of caring.